BEST OF

Pillsbury

Bake-Off®

casseroles

JG
PRESS

Published by World Publications Group, Inc., 140 Laurel Street, East Bridgewater, MA 02333, www.wrldpub.com

Library of Congress Cataloging-in-Publication Data is available upon request.

ISBN: 978-1-4643-0103-2

Printed in China

10 9 8 7 6 5 4 3 2 1

Cover photo: Taco Biscuit Casserole (page 10)

GENERAL MILLS

Editorial Director
Jeff Nowak

Publishing Manager
Christine Gray

Manager, Cookbooks
Lois Tlusty

Editors
Lori Fox and Grace Wells

Recipe Development and Testing
Pillsbury Kitchens

Photography
General Mills Photography Studios and Image Library

Photographer
Val Bourassa

Food Stylists
Nancy Johnson

JOHN WILEY & SONS, INC.

Publisher
Natalie Chapman

Associate Publisher
Jessica Goodman

Executive Editor
Anne Ficklen

Assistant Editor
Charleen Barila

Production
Alda Trabucchi and Kristi Hart

Cover Design
Suzanne Sunwoo

Art Director
Tai Blanche

Interior Design and Layout
Holly Wittenberg

Photography Art Direction
Chris Everett/See Design, Inc.

Prop Stylist
Michelle Joy

Manufacturing Manager
Kevin Watt

Our recipes have been tested in the Pillsbury Kitchens and meet our standards of easy preparation, reliability and great taste.

For more great recipes, visit pillsbury.com

contents

the Bake-Off® contest through the years   4

casseroles through the decades   7

1   hearty beef favorites   9

2   savory pork suppers   51

3   comforting chicken & turkey   75

4   seafood & meatless mainstays   103

5   dinner pies & quiches   127

helpful nutrition and cooking information   152

metric conversion guide   153

index   154

There is nothing like the Pillsbury Bake-Off® Contest.

Have you ever made something so good that you just had to share it? Or tweaked a recipe until it was just right? Or nervously waited as the family took the first bite of a new dish?

Then you've experienced a Bake-Off Contest.

Like everyday cooks around the country, Pillsbury Bake-Off winners envisioned making a dish so yummy that family and friends would ask for more.

Of course, the Bake-Off Contest is a little different. A panel of judges try that first bite. Ninety-nine other cooks share "your" kitchen. But the pay-off for your great recipe is a million times more lucrative than usual.

Whether you're a finalist at a Pillsbury Bake-Off Contest or simply a star in your own kitchen, you share something special. Both you and Bake-Off contestants know the food you developed with love for your family will become treasured family recipes in someone's home.

1950s

The first Pillsbury Bake-Off Contest spurred a phenomenon that many copied but few have perfected over the years. Throughout the '50s, the annual Bake-Off Contest showcased the creativity of America's best home cooks and their favorite new flavors in the kitchen. The fictitious everywoman, Ann Pillsbury—aka The Pillsbury Lady—presided over the contest and its innovative magazines. Ann encouraged cooks young and old to share a "love of good baked things that is so very strong in our country." Reflecting mid-century interest in the glamorous home, the contest was held at New York City's Waldorf-Astoria Hotel where it resided for many years. The contest showcased kitchen innovations including a white General Electric four-burner, double-oven. By the late '50s, electric mixers, another labor- and time-saving device, were introduced in each cook's "kitchen" at the contest. In the early years, every recipe included Pillsbury BEST® enriched flour.

1960s

In the '60s, the "Busy Lady" was a Bake-Off theme. Bake-Off recipes were "shortcutted, streamlined and up-to-dated for you" by Pillsbury. Although the heart of the home was still the kitchen in the '60s, the fact that many women led busy lives outside of the kitchen meant everyday cooks created easy but delicious meals for their families. While it "used to take all day to make a bread," the prizewinning Chicken Little Bread promised a great homemade loaf in less time. In 1967, the official Bake-Off magazine featured shortcuts to prize recipes and offered "homemade goodness with hurry-up timing" to the average family cook. At the Bake-Off Contest, the self-cleaning oven made its debut, and fresh refrigerated biscuit and crescent roll doughs were used as key ingredients for the first time. In 1969, the contest changed forever when it introduced "three divisions"—flour, mix and fresh refrigerated dough—each with a $10,000 Grand Prize. The best recipe won a $25,000 cash prize.

1970s

By 1972, Ann Pillsbury had disappeared from the Bake-Off Contest, but a new icon had taken her place. The Pillsbury Doughboy, in a cowboy hat, graced the cover of the 1972 Bake-Off recipe collection. His friendly face would remain a standing symbol of the contest for some time to come. The Doughboy's cowboy hat symbolized more than a friendly demeanor. It signaled the Bake-Off Contest was on the move. Houston, New Orleans, San Diego and San Francisco were new sites for the contest and reflected America's growing diversity and shifts in population away from the East Coast. Celebrity hosts and judges awarded prizes on Bake-Off day. By the early '70s, the "health" food craze was recognizable in the Bake-Off Contest. Many recipes featured apples, carrots, whole wheat, oats and granola, but most contestant recipes reflected a lack of time for cooking. In the mid-'70s, the Bake-Off recipe collection cost around a dollar and included recipes developed for the newest kitchen innovation, the microwave oven.

1980s

In the mid-'80s, the Bake-Off Contest offered a fast-forward cuisine of quick and easy recipes, snacks and a new entrant to the arena, ethnic recipes. Competitors brought a wide variety of ethnic backgrounds to the contest. Wontons and Mexican-style recipes popped on the Bake-Off scene for the first time. The microwave acquired a place in almost every home in the '80s, and many finalists used a microwave to prepare part or all of their entries in a matter of minutes. A microwave category was a new category at the contest. High-spending style was a hallmark of the '80s, and the Bake-Off Contest followed suit. The Grand Prize increased to $40,000, and first-place winners in each of five categories won $15,000 for their favorite family recipes. Celebrities continued to be featured hosts, and in 1983, Bob Barker, longtime host of the TV show *The Price Is Right*, awarded more than $130,000 in cash prizes in San Diego.

1990s

Although the theme "quick and easy" had been a staple at past Bake-Off Contests, for the first time in 1998, Quick & Easy was its own category in the contest, increasing the number of Bake-Off categories to five. The categories—30-Minute Main Dishes, Simple Side Dishes, Fast and Easy Treats, and Quick Snacks and Appetizers—all reflected the changing nature of the American kitchen. What changed in the kitchen? Time, more than ever, was in short supply for families with jobs, hobbies and kids, but a desire to give families the best food that mom—or dad—could make was never compromised by Bake-Off contestants. The contest entered the modern era on February 26, 1996, when more than $1,054,000 in cash and prizes were awarded for the first time. The first million-dollar winner was Macadamia Fudge Torte, a recipe developed by Kurt Wait of California, one of 14 men whose recipes were chosen for the contest.

2000s

At the turn of the century, the Bake-Off Contest turned 50! After all these years, the contest is still about creating great food while reflecting the changing nature of American society. In the first decade of the new century, the Bake-Off Contest offered adventurous flavors that blurred ethnic boundaries. Bolder, even exotic, flavors came to the forefront as American cooks encountered a variety of cooking styles both at home and in travels around the world. For the first time, recipes could be entered into the contest in Spanish. In 2006 and 2008, a new Bake-Off prize was added—America's Favorite Recipe. Consumers voted online for their favorite recipe among the final 100 recipes. The recipe that received the most online votes received the America's Favorite Recipe Award and a cash prize.

Recipes entered in the Pillsbury Bake-Off® Contest through the years reveal what flavors were popular, the ingredients found in most pantries, the changing demographics of our country and what was happening in households nationwide.

1950s

Entrées have been a Bake-Off Contest category since the very first contest, and the most popular entrées were casseroles. The main dishes of this era could best be described as hearty and satisfying. The first time an entrée recipe was awarded Grand Prize was at the 8th Bake-Off Contest held in 1956. California Casserole, a veal casserole topped with dumplings, was the winning recipe.

Popular '50s Bake-Off® casserole recipe:
California Casserole

1960s

During the '60s, more women joined the workforce and began making strides in their professional careers. With less time to cook, women looked for easier, less complicated recipes, and there was an increase in use of convenience foods and time-saving methods. Refrigerated crescent rolls and biscuits were new at the time and became popular ingredients in main dish entries.

Popular '60s Bake-Off® casserole recipes:
- Hungry Boys' Casserole
- Crafty Crescent Lasagna
- Cheeseburger Casserole

1970s

Health and nutrition occupied the minds of home cooks in the '70s, and there was a definite trend to include broccoli, zucchini, spinach, carrots and every kind of bean in main dish recipes. Overall, casserole recipes were inexpensive to make and streamlined steps made them easy to prepare. Twists to Mexican dishes were very popular.

Popular '70s Bake-Off® casserole recipes:
- Zesty Italian Crescent Casserole
- Savory Crust Chicken Bake
- Easy Enchilada Bake

1980s

Two-paycheck families became a necessity in the '80s, creating more demand for simple main dish recipes. Recipes with Mexican and Tex-Mex flavors continued to be popular, along with Italian-inspired recipes. In ethnic entries, traditional ingredients were used with a convenience product that replaced made-from-scratch dough or pastry. Chicken became more common than red meat in main dish recipes.

Popular '80s Bake-Off® casserole recipes:
- Chicken and Cheese Crescent Chimichangas
- Fiesta Chicken Casserole
- Biscuit-Topped Italian Casserole

◄ *Savory Crescent Chicken Squares (page 97)*

1990s

In the '90s, recipes reflected the increasingly global community and pantries were more internationalized, stocked with ingredients once considered exotic, like coconut milk, 5-spice powder, couscous and sun-dried tomatoes. Consumers discovered the health benefits of legumes, and by the late '90s, a popular vegetable was canned black beans. There also was an increase in vegetarian main dishes.

Popular '90s Bake-Off® casserole recipes:
- Black Bean and Cheese Tortilla Pie
- Tamale Casserole
- Chicken Suiza Corn Bread Bake

2000s

Television cooking shows with celebrity chefs and food-oriented web sites soared in popularity, and home cooks incorporated cooking techniques learned from these resources into their recipes. Bake-Off® Contest entries ranged from long and involved to quick and easy. To save time, many main dish recipes used quick and easy ingredients, like rotisserie chicken and pre-washed and cut produce.

Popular 2000s Bake-Off® casserole recipes:
- Turkey–Sweet Potato Pot Pies
- Pineapple–Black Bean Enchiladas
- Poblanos Florentine Casserole

Taco Biscuit Casserole (page 10) ▶

taco biscuit casserole

KAREN HAMILTON
Titonka, IA
Bake-Off® Contest 39, 2000

8 SERVINGS
PREP TIME: *15 minutes*
START TO FINISH: *50 minutes*

CASSEROLE

1½ lb lean (at least 80%) ground beef

1 package (1 oz) taco seasoning mix

¾ cup water

1¼ cups chunky-style salsa

1 can (16.3 oz) Pillsbury® Grands!® Flaky Layers or Homestyle refrigerated buttermilk biscuits

2 cups shredded Mexican cheese blend (8 oz)

TOPPINGS, AS DESIRED

Shredded lettuce

Chopped tomatoes

Additional chunky-style salsa

Sliced ripe olives, drained

Sour cream

Sliced green onions

1 Heat oven to 375°F. In 10-inch skillet, cook beef over medium-high heat 9 to 10 minutes, stirring frequently, until thoroughly cooked; drain. Stir in taco seasoning mix, water and salsa; heat to boiling. Reduce heat; simmer uncovered 3 minutes, stirring occasionally, while preparing biscuits. Remove from heat.

2 Separate dough into 8 biscuits. Cut each biscuit into 8 pieces. Add pieces to beef mixture; stir gently. Spoon mixture into ungreased 13 × 9-inch pan.

3 Bake 18 to 23 minutes or until sauce is bubbly and biscuits are golden brown. Sprinkle with cheese. Bake 8 to 10 minutes longer or until cheese is bubbly. To serve, cut into 8 squares. Top with toppings.

High Altitude (3500–6500 ft): No change.

Photo on page 9.

1 Serving (Without Toppings): Calories 440; Total Fat 25g (Saturated Fat 11g; Trans Fat 4g); Cholesterol 80mg; Sodium 1370mg; Total Carbohydrate 29g (Dietary Fiber 1g) **Exchanges:** 1½ Starch, ½ Other Carbohydrate, 3 High-Fat Meat **Carbohydrate Choices:** 2

easy enchilada bake

4 SERVINGS

PREP TIME: *15 minutes*

START TO FINISH: *45 minutes*

MISS AMY STAUFENBIEL

St. Louis, MO

Bake-Off® Contest 21, 1970

1 Heat oven to 350°F.

2 In 10-inch skillet, cook beef over medium heat 8 to 10 minutes, stirring occasionally, until thoroughly cooked; drain. Stir in garlic, ⅓ cup of the onions (reserve remaining onions for filling), the water, barbecue sauce, chili powder and salt. Heat to boiling. Reduce heat; simmer uncovered 5 minutes, stirring occasionally, while preparing biscuits.

3 Sprinkle cornmeal on work surface. Separate dough into 10 biscuits. Coat both sides of biscuits with cornmeal; roll or pat into 5-inch rounds. Place 1 tablespoon cheese and 1 tablespoon onions down center of each round; roll up, placing seam-side down in ungreased 12 × 8-inch (2-quart) glass baking dish or 9-inch square (2-quart) glass baking dish. Cover with warm meat mixture. Sprinkle with any remaining cheese and onions.*

4 Bake 25 to 30 minutes or until cheese is melted and centers of biscuits are no longer doughy.

*To make ahead, prepare, cover and refrigerate up to 2 hours before baking. Bake as directed.

High Altitude (3500–6500 ft): No change.

1 to 1¼ lb lean (at least 80%) ground beef

1 clove garlic, finely chopped, or ⅛ teaspoon instant minced garlic

1 to 1⅓ cups chopped onions

¾ cup water

½ cup barbecue sauce

½ to 1 tablespoon chili powder

½ teaspoon salt

Cornmeal

1 can (7.5 oz) Pillsbury refrigerated buttermilk or Country® biscuits

2 cups shredded Cheddar cheese (8 oz)

1 Serving: Calories 680; Total Fat 37g (Saturated Fat 18g; Trans Fat 1.5g); Cholesterol 145mg; Sodium 1550mg; Total Carbohydrate 44g (Dietary Fiber 2g) **Exchanges:** 3 Starch, 4½ Medium-Fat Meat, 2 Fat **Carbohydrate Choices:** 3

beef 'n beans with cheesy biscuits

MRS. O. A. CREED

Florissant, MO

Bake-Off® Contest 22, 1971

5 SERVINGS

PREP TIME: *15 minutes*

START TO FINISH: *40 minutes*

1 lb lean (at least 80%) ground beef

½ cup chopped onion

1 can (16 oz) baked beans, barbecue beans or pork and beans with molasses, undrained

1 can (10¾ oz) condensed tomato soup

1 teaspoon chili powder

¼ teaspoon garlic powder

1 can (7.5 oz) Pillsbury refrigerated buttermilk or Country biscuits

1 cup shredded Cheddar or American cheese (4 oz)

1 Heat oven to 375°F. In 10-inch skillet, cook beef and onion over medium-high heat 5 to 7 minutes, stirring frequently, until beef is thoroughly cooked; drain.

2 Stir in beans, soup, chili powder and garlic powder. Heat to boiling. Reduce heat; simmer uncovered 5 minutes, stirring occasionally, while preparing biscuits.

3 Separate dough into 10 biscuits. Spoon hot beef mixture into ungreased 8-inch square (2-quart) glass baking dish or 2-quart casserole. Arrange biscuits over hot mixture. Sprinkle with cheese.

4 Bake 20 to 25 minutes or until mixture is bubbly and biscuits are golden brown and no longer doughy.

High Altitude (3500–6500 ft): Do not sprinkle with cheese in step 3. In step 4, bake 15 minutes; sprinkle with cheese. Bake 5 to 10 minutes longer.

1 Serving: Calories 480; Total Fat 20g (Saturated Fat 9g; Trans Fat 1g); Cholesterol 80mg; Sodium 1570mg; Total Carbohydrate 44g (Dietary Fiber 5g) **Exchanges:** 2 Starch, 1 Other Carbohydrate, 3½ Medium-Fat Meat **Carbohydrate Choices:** 3

zesty biscuit bean bake

MRS. MAUREEN ERICKSON
Duluth, MN
Bake-Off® Contest 27, 1976

6 SERVINGS
PREP TIME: *15 minutes*
START TO FINISH: *35 minutes*

1 lb lean (at least 80%) ground beef

¼ cup chopped onion or 1 tablespoon instant minced onion

1 package (1.31 oz) sloppy joe seasoning mix

2 cans (16 oz each) baked beans or pork and beans, undrained

2 to 4 tablespoons packed brown sugar

½ cup ketchup

1 can (12 oz) Pillsbury Grands! Jr. Golden Layers® refrigerated biscuits

15 oz Cheddar or American Cheese, cut into 10 (½-inch) cubes

1 Heat oven to 375°F. In 10-inch ovenproof or cast-iron skillet, cook beef and onion over medium heat 8 to 10 minutes, stirring occasionally, until thoroughly cooked; drain. Measure 1 tablespoon seasoning mix. Place in small bowl; set aside. Add remaining seasoning mix, beans, brown sugar and ketchup to beef; heat until hot and bubbly.*

2 Separate dough into 10 biscuits. Place cheese cube in center of each biscuit. Fold dough over cheese, covering completely; seal well, shaping into balls. Roll each biscuit in remaining seasoning mix to coat; arrange biscuits on hot meat mixture.

3 Bake 20 to 25 minutes or until deep golden brown.

*If you don't have an ovenproof skillet, pour hot beef mixture into ungreased 12 × 8-inch glass baking dish or shallow 3-quart casserole. Top with biscuits and bake as directed.

High Altitude (3500–6500 ft): No change.

1 Serving: Calories 790; Total Fat 39g (Saturated Fat 19g; Trans Fat 3.5g); Cholesterol 115mg; Sodium 2850mg; Total Carbohydrate 71g (Dietary Fiber 6g) **Exchanges:** 2½ Starch, 2 Other Carbohydrate, 4½ Medium-Fat Meat, 3 Fat **Carbohydrate Choices:** 5

cheesy beef 'n crescent bake

6 SERVINGS
PREP TIME: *20 minutes*
START TO FINISH: *50 minutes*

MRS. KIRSTEN H. RINDONE
Chula Vista, CA
Bake-Off® Contest 22, 1971

1 Heat oven to 375°F. In 10-inch skillet, cook beef, onion, salt and pepper over medium heat 9 to 11 minutes, stirring occasionally, until beef is thoroughly cooked; drain. Stir in soup, milk and peas. Reduce heat; simmer uncovered, stirring occasionally, while preparing cheese mixture.

2 In small bowl, mix cheese and pimientos; set aside. Separate dough into 4 rectangles. Firmly press perforations to seal. Spread each rectangle with 2 generous tablespoons cheese mixture. Starting at longer side, roll up each rectangle. Cut each roll into 4 pieces, forming 16 rolls.

3 Into ungreased 2-quart casserole or 8- or 9-inch square pan, pour hot beef mixture. Arrange rolls, cut side down, evenly over beef mixture.

4 Bake 25 to 30 minutes until golden brown.

High Altitude (3500–6500 ft): Bake 27 to 32 minutes.

1 to 1¼ lb lean (at least 80%) ground beef

½ cup chopped onion or 2 tablespoons instant minced onion

½ teaspoon salt

Dash pepper

1 can (10¾ oz) condensed Cheddar cheese soup

½ cup milk

2 cups frozen sweet peas, cooked, drained or 1 can (15 oz) sweet peas, drained

1 cup shredded Cheddar or American cheese (4 oz)

1 jar (2 oz) diced pimientos, drained

1 can (8 oz) Pillsbury refrigerated crescent dinner rolls

1 Serving: Calories 450; Total Fat 27g (Saturated Fat 12g; Trans Fat 3.5g); Cholesterol 75mg; Sodium 1140mg; Total Carbohydrate 27g (Dietary Fiber 2g) **Exchanges:** 1 Starch, ½ Other Carbohydrate, ½ Vegetable, 3 Lean Meat, 3½ Fat **Carbohydrate Choices:** 2

chuck wagon cheeseburger skillet

ROSEMARY WARMUTH

Wheeling, WV

Bake-Off® Contest 40, 2002

5 SERVINGS

PREP TIME: *15 minutes*

START TO FINISH: *40 minutes*

4 slices bacon

1 lb lean (at least 80%) ground beef

3 tablespoons chopped onion

3 tablespoons vegetable oil

2½ cups frozen hash-brown potatoes, thawed

1 can (11 oz) whole kernel corn with red and green peppers, drained

1 can (4.5 oz) chopped green chiles, drained

½ cup barbecue sauce

2 cups shredded Cheddar cheese (8 oz)

¼ teaspoon salt, if desired

¼ teaspoon pepper, if desired

1 can (16.3 oz) Pillsbury Grands! refrigerated buttermilk biscuits or reduced fat buttermilk biscuits

1 Heat oven to 400°F. Cook bacon until crisp. Drain on paper towel; crumble. Set aside.

2 In 12-inch cast-iron or ovenproof skillet, cook beef and onion over medium heat 8 to 10 minutes, stirring occasionally, until beef is thoroughly cooked; drain. Place beef mixture in medium bowl; cover to keep warm.

3 In same skillet, heat oil over medium-high heat until hot. Add potatoes; cook 3 to 5 minutes, stirring constantly, until browned. Add cooked beef and remaining ingredients except biscuits; mix well. Cook until hot, stirring occasionally. Sprinkle with bacon. Leave on heat so mixture is hot when adding biscuits.

4 Separate dough into 8 biscuits. Arrange biscuits over hot mixture.

5 Bake 16 to 24 minutes or until biscuits are deep golden brown and bottoms are no longer doughy.

High Altitude (3500–6500 ft): No change.

1 Serving: Calories 940; Total Fat 50g (Saturated Fat 20g; Trans Fat 6g); Cholesterol 110mg; Sodium 2280mg; Total Carbohydrate 83g (Dietary Fiber 4g) **Exchanges:** 3½ Starch, 2 Other Carbohydrate, 4 Medium-Fat Meat, 5½ Fat **Carbohydrate Choices:** 5½

cheeseburger casserole

RICHARD KLECKA
Tinley Park, IL
Bake-Off® Contest 14, 1962

5 SERVINGS
PREP TIME: *25 minutes*
START TO FINISH: *45 minutes*

1 lb lean (at least 80%) ground beef

⅓ cup chopped onion

½ teaspoon salt

⅛ teaspoon pepper

1 can (10¾ oz) condensed tomato soup

1 cup frozen sweet peas (from 12-oz bag)

½ cup water

1 can (7.5 oz) Pillsbury refrigerated buttermilk or Country biscuits

3 oz American or Cheddar cheese, cut into 10 (¾-inch) cubes

1 Heat oven to 400°F. In 10-inch skillet, cook beef, onion, salt and pepper over medium-high heat 5 to 7 minutes, stirring frequently, until beef is thoroughly cooked; drain.

2 Stir in soup, peas and water. Heat to boiling, about 3 minutes. Reduce heat; simmer 5 minutes, stirring occasionally, while preparing biscuits.

3 Separate dough into 10 biscuits. Wrap each biscuit around cheese cube, pinching edges to seal.

4 Place beef mixture in ungreased 1½-quart round casserole. Arrange cheese-filled biscuits, seam side down, in single layer over hot mixture.

5 Bake 13 to 18 minutes or until biscuits are golden brown.

High Altitude (3500–6500 ft): Use 2-quart round casserole. Bake 18 to 23 minutes.

1 Serving: Calories 400; Total Fat 18g (Saturated Fat 7g; Trans Fat 1g); Cholesterol 70mg; Sodium 1310mg; Total Carbohydrate 34g (Dietary Fiber 2g) **Exchanges:** 1 Starch, 1 Other Carbohydrate, 3 Medium-Fat Meat, 1 Fat **Carbohydrate Choices:** 2

cheesy biscuit chili casserole

5 SERVINGS

PREP TIME: *20 minutes*

START TO FINISH: *45 minutes*

MRS. OTTO NEYHOUSE
Oakland City, IN
Bake-Off® Contest 22, 1971

1 Heat oven to 375°F. In 10-inch skillet, cook beef and onion over medium heat 8 to 10 minutes, stirring occasionally, until beef is thoroughly cooked; drain. Measure 2½ tablespoons seasoning mix; set aside. Stir remaining seasoning mix, cheese and water into beef mixture; remove ½ cup beef mixture; set aside. Stir barbecue sauce into remaining beef mixture. Reduce heat; simmer uncovered while preparing dough.

2 Separate dough into 10 biscuits. Press biscuits together to form a rectangle about 9 × 7 inches; spread reserved ½ cup beef mixture over dough. Overlap long sides of rectangle over beef mixture; cut into 12 slices. Into ungreased 8- or 9-inch square pan or 2-quart casserole, spoon remaining hot beef mixture. Arrange biscuit slices, cut side down, in a circle around edge of pan. In small bowl, mix topping ingredients with whisk or fork; pour evenly over biscuits.

3 Bake 25 to 30 minutes or until golden brown and biscuits are no longer doughy.

High Altitude (3500–6500 ft): No change.

CASSEROLE
1¼ to 1½ lb lean (at least 80%) ground beef

⅓ cup chopped onion or 2 tablespoons instant minced onion

1 package (1.25 oz) chili seasoning mix

1 cup shredded Cheddar or American cheese (4 oz)

¼ cup water

½ cup barbecue sauce

1 can (7.5 oz) Pillsbury refrigerated buttermilk or Country biscuits

TOPPING
1 egg

¼ cup milk

½ cup shredded Cheddar or American cheese (2 oz)

1 Serving: Calories 540; Total Fat 27g (Saturated Fat 12g; Trans Fat 1g); Cholesterol 150mg; Sodium 1310mg; Total Carbohydrate 39g (Dietary Fiber 3g) **Exchanges:** 2 Starch, ½ Other Carbohydrate, 3 Lean Meat, 1 High-Fat Meat, 1½ Fat **Carbohydrate Choices:** 2½

three cheese 'n beef biscuit casserole

MRS. MEHRL D. FEEHAN
New Orleans, LA
Bake-Off® Contest 23, 1972

6 SERVINGS
PREP TIME: *30 minutes*
START TO FINISH: *45 minutes*

CASSEROLE

1 lb lean (at least 80%) ground beef

1 can (6 oz) tomato paste

2 tablespoons olive or vegetable oil

1 package (1.5 oz) spaghetti sauce mix

½ teaspoon salt

½ teaspoon pepper

½ teaspoon garlic powder

1 tablespoon butter or margarine

¼ cup sliced ripe olives, if desired

1 can (7.5 oz) Pillsbury refrigerated
  buttermilk or Country biscuits

Grated Parmesan cheese

FILLING

1½ cups shredded mozzarella cheese
  (6 oz)

½ cup ricotta or cottage cheese

1 tablespoon chopped fresh or
  1 teaspoon parsley flakes

1 tablespoon chopped fresh or
  ½ teaspoon freeze-dried chives

1 tablespoon chopped fresh or
  ½ teaspoon dried basil leaves

1 Heat oven to 400°F. In 10-inch skillet, cook beef over medium heat 8 to 10 minutes, stirring occasionally, until thoroughly cooked; drain. Add tomato paste, oil, spaghetti sauce mix and amount of water as directed on sauce mix package. Heat to boiling. Stir in salt, pepper, garlic powder, butter and olives. Reduce heat; simmer uncovered 10 minutes, stirring occasionally, while preparing biscuits.

2 Separate dough into 10 biscuits. Pat or roll each biscuit into a 4-inch round. In small bowl, mix filling ingredients. Spoon about 2 tablespoons filling onto each round. Fold biscuit in half; seal edges well.

3 Into ungreased 13 × 9-inch (3-quart) baking dish, pour half of hot beef mixture. Top with filled biscuits. Pour remaining beef mixture around biscuits. Sprinkle generously with Parmesan cheese.

4 Bake 15 to 25 minutes or until golden brown.

High Altitude (3500–6500 ft): No change.

1 Serving: Calories 440; Total Fat 24g (Saturated Fat 10g; Trans Fat 1g); Cholesterol 75mg; Sodium 1570mg; Total Carbohydrate 29g (Dietary Fiber 2g) **Exchanges:** 1½ Starch, 1 Vegetable, 2 Lean Meat, 1 High-Fat Meat, 2 Fat **Carbohydrate Choices:** 2

beefed-up biscuit casserole

5 SERVINGS

PREP TIME: *15 minutes*
START TO FINISH: *40 minutes*

CLAUDIA LYNN STAFFORD
Ames, IA
Bake-Off® Contest 22, 1971

1 Heat oven to 375°F. In 10-inch skillet, cook beef, onion and chiles over medium heat 8 to 10 minutes, stirring occasionally, until beef is thoroughly cooked; drain. Stir in tomato sauce, chili powder and garlic salt. Heat to boiling. Reduce heat; simmer uncovered, stirring occasionally, while preparing dough.

2 Separate dough into 10 biscuits. Separate each biscuit into 2 layers. In bottom of ungreased 8- or 9-inch square pan, press 10 biscuit layers. Mix ½ cup of the cheese (reserve remaining cheese for topping), the sour cream and egg.

3 Remove beef mixture from heat; stir in sour cream mixture. Spoon beef mixture over biscuit layer in pan. Arrange remaining biscuit layers on top; sprinkle with remaining1 cup cheese.*

4 Bake 25 to 30 minutes until biscuits are deep golden brown.

*To make ahead, prepare, cover and refrigerate up to 2 hours before baking. Bake as directed.

High Altitude (3500–6500 ft): No change.

1 to 1¼ lb (at least 80%) ground beef
½ cup chopped onion or 2 tablespoons instant minced onion
¼ cup diced green chiles or green bell pepper
1 can (8 oz) tomato sauce
2 teaspoons chili powder
½ to ¾ teaspoon garlic salt
1 can (7.5 oz) Pillsbury refrigerated buttermilk or Country biscuits
1½ cups shredded Monterey Jack or Cheddar cheese (6 oz)
½ cup sour cream
1 egg, slightly beaten

1 Serving: Calories 470; Total Fat 28g (Saturated Fat 13g; Trans Fat 1g); Cholesterol 145mg; Sodium 990mg; Total Carbohydrate 26g (Dietary Fiber 2g) **Exchanges:** 1½ Starch, ½ Vegetable, 2 Lean Meat, 1½ High-Fat Meat, 1½ Fat **Carbohydrate Choices:** 2

hungry boys' casserole

MIRA WALILKO
Detroit, MI
Bake-Off® Contest 15, 1963

8 SERVINGS
PREP TIME: *40 minutes*
START TO FINISH: *1 hour 5 minutes*

CASSEROLE

1½ lb lean (at least 80%) ground beef
1 cup chopped celery
½ cup chopped onion
½ cup chopped green bell pepper
1 garlic clove, finely chopped
1 can (6 oz) tomato paste
¾ cup water
1 teaspoon paprika
½ teaspoon salt
1 can (16 oz) baked beans, undrained
1 can (15 oz) garbanzo beans
   or chick peas, undrained

BISCUITS

1½ cups Pillsbury BEST® all-purpose
   or unbleached flour
2 teaspoons baking powder
½ teaspoon salt
¼ cup butter or margarine
½ to ¾ cup milk
2 tablespoons sliced stuffed
   green olives
1 tablespoon slivered almonds

1 In 12-inch skillet, cook beef, celery, onion, bell pepper and garlic over medium-high heat 9 to 10 minutes, stirring frequently, until beef is thoroughly cooked and vegetables are crisp-tender; drain. Reduce heat to low. Stir in tomato paste, water, paprika and ½ teaspoon salt. Add baked beans and garbanzo beans. Simmer uncovered, stirring occasionally, while preparing biscuits.

2 Heat oven to 425°F. In large bowl, mix flour, baking powder and ½ teaspoon salt. Cut in butter, using pastry blender (or pulling 2 table knives through mixture in opposite directions) until mixture looks like coarse crumbs. Gradually stir in enough milk until mixture leaves sides of bowl and forms a soft, moist dough.

3 On floured surface, gently knead dough 8 times. Roll dough ¼ inch thick. Cut with floured 2½-inch doughnut cutter. Reserve dough centers. Reroll dough to cut additional biscuits.

4 Reserve ½ cup of hot beef mixture. Pour remaining beef mixture into ungreased 13 × 9-inch (3-quart) glass baking dish. Arrange biscuits without centers over beef mixture. Stir olives and almonds into reserved ½ cup beef mixture; spoon into center of each biscuit. Top each with biscuit centers.

5 Bake 15 to 25 minutes or until biscuits are golden brown.

High Altitude (3500–6500 ft): No change.

1 Serving: Calories 460; Total Fat 18g (Saturated Fat 8g; Trans Fat 1g); Cholesterol 75mg; Sodium 1020mg; Total Carbohydrate 47g (Dietary Fiber 8g) **Exchanges:** 2½ Starch, ½ Other Carbohydrate, 2½ Medium-Fat Meat, 1 Fat **Carbohydrate Choices:** 3

biscuit-topped italian casserole

ROBERT WICK
Altamonte Springs, FL
Bake-Off® Contest 33, 1988

10 SERVINGS

PREP TIME: *50 minutes*

START TO FINISH: *1 hour 20 minutes*

1 tablespoon vegetable oil, if desired

1 lb lean (at least 80%) ground beef

½ cup chopped onion

¾ cup water

½ teaspoon salt, if desired

¼ teaspoon pepper

1 can (8 oz) tomato sauce

1 can (6 oz) tomato paste

2 cups shredded mozzarella cheese (8 oz)

1½ cups frozen mixed vegetables, thawed

2 cans (12 oz each) Pillsbury Grands! Jr. Golden Layers refrigerated biscuits

1 tablespoon butter or margarine, melted

½ teaspoon dried oregano leaves, crushed

1 Heat oven to 375°F. Grease or spray 13 × 9-inch (3-quart) glass baking dish.

2 In 10-inch skillet, heat oil over medium heat until hot. Cook beef and onion in oil 8 to 10 minutes, stirring occasionally, until beef is thoroughly cooked; drain. Stir in water, salt, pepper, tomato sauce and tomato paste. Heat to boiling. Reduce heat; simmer uncovered 15 minutes, stirring occasionally

3 Place half of meat mixture in baking dish; sprinkle with ⅔ cup of the cheese. Spoon mixed vegetables evenly over cheese; sprinkle an additional ⅔ cup cheese over vegetables. Spoon remaining hot meat mixture evenly over cheese and vegetables; sprinkle with remaining ⅔ cup cheese.

4 Separate dough into 20 biscuits. Separate each biscuit into 3 layers. Arrange layers over hot meat mixture, overlapping, in 3 rows of 20 layers each. Gently brush biscuits with butter; sprinkle with oregano.

5 Bake 22 to 27 minutes or until biscuit topping is golden brown.

High Altitude (3500–6500 ft): Bake 27 to 32 minutes.

1 Serving: Calories 410; Total Fat 20g (Saturated Fat 8g; Trans Fat 3.5g); Cholesterol 45mg; Sodium 1130mg; Total Carbohydrate 38g (Dietary Fiber 3g) **Exchanges:** 2 Starch, ½ Other Carbohydrate, 2 Medium-Fat Meat, 1½ Fat **Carbohydrate Choices:** 2½

beef 'n bean biscuit casserole

5 SERVINGS

PREP TIME: *20 minutes*

START TO FINISH: *50 minutes*

MRS. BETTY JUDY
Rockville, MD
Bake-Off® Contest 23, 1972

1 Heat oven to 350°F. In 10-inch skillet, cook beef, celery and bell pepper over medium heat 8 to 10 minutes, stirring occasionally, until beef is thoroughly cooked; drain. Stir in beans, barbecue sauce, jelly and salt; continue to cook until hot. Meanwhile, in 6-inch skillet, melt butter over medium heat; cook onion in butter until light brown. Stir in pimientos.

2 Separate dough into 10 biscuits. On work surface, press biscuits together to make 9 × 7-inch rectangle. Spread onion-pimiento mixture over dough. Starting at longer side, roll up rectangle, pressing edges to seal. Cut roll into nine 1-inch slices. Into ungreased 8-inch square (2-quart) glass baking dish, spoon beef mixture. Top with biscuit pinwheels.

3 Bake 25 to 30 minutes or until golden brown.

High Altitude (3500–6500 ft): Heat oven to 375°F.

1 lb lean (at least 80%) ground beef

1 cup chopped celery

¼ cup chopped green bell pepper

1 can (16 oz) baked beans or pork and beans, undrained

½ cup barbecue sauce

½ cup grape jelly

1 teaspoon salt

1 tablespoon butter or margarine

½ cup chopped onion or 2 tablespoons instant minced onion

1 tablespoon chopped pimientos

1 can (7.5 oz) Pillsbury refrigerated buttermilk or Country biscuits

1 Serving: Calories 520; Total Fat 14g (Saturated Fat 5g; Trans Fat 1g); Cholesterol 60mg; Sodium 1530mg; Total Carbohydrate 73g (Dietary Fiber 5g) **Exchanges:** 2½ Starch, 2 Other Carbohydrate, ½ Vegetable, 2 Lean Meat, 1½ Fat **Carbohydrate Choices:** 5

zesty italian crescent casserole

MADELLA BATHKE
Wells, MN
Bake-Off® Contest 28, 1978

6 SERVINGS
PREP TIME: *15 minutes*
START TO FINISH: *40 minutes*

1 lb lean (at least 80%) ground beef

¼ cup chopped onion or 1 tablespoon instant minced onion

1 package (1.5 oz) spaghetti sauce mix

1 can (8 oz) tomato sauce

1½ cups shredded mozzarella or Monterey Jack cheese (6 oz)

½ cup sour cream

1 can (8 oz) Pillsbury refrigerated crescent dinner rolls

⅓ cup grated Parmesan cheese

2 tablespoons butter or margarine, melted

1 Heat oven to 375°F. In 10-inch skillet, cook beef and onion over medium heat 8 to 10 minutes, stirring occasionally, until beef is thoroughly cooked; drain. Stir in sauce mix and tomato sauce; heat until hot and bubbly. In small bowl, mix cheese and sour cream. Pour hot meat mixture into ungreased 12 × 8-inch (2-quart) or 13 × 9-inch (3-quart) glass baking dish. Spoon cheese mixture over meat.

2 Separate dough into two rectangles. Place rectangles over cheese mixture. In small bowl, mix Parmesan cheese and butter; crumble evenly over dough.

3 Bake 18 to 25 minutes or until deep golden brown. Cut into squares to serve.

High Altitude (3500–6500 ft): No change.

1 Serving: Calories 490; Total Fat 31g (Saturated Fat 15g; Trans Fat 3g); Cholesterol 90mg; Sodium 1390mg; Total Carbohydrate 24g (Dietary Fiber 1g) **Exchanges:** 1½ Starch, 3 Medium-Fat Meat, 3 Fat **Carbohydrate Choices:** 1½

smoky southwestern shepherd's pie

KRISTINA VANNI
Libertyville, IL
Bake-Off® Contest 39, 2000

6 SERVINGS
PREP TIME: *15 minutes*
START TO FINISH: *40 minutes*

1½ lb lean (at least 80%) ground beef
½ cup chopped onion
2 cups water
3 tablespoons butter or margarine
½ teaspoon salt
¾ cup milk
2 cups mashed potato flakes
1 can (4.5 oz) chopped green chiles
1 cup shredded Mexican cheese
    blend (4 oz)
1 can (10 oz) enchilada sauce
1 to 2 canned chipotle chiles in
    adobo sauce (from 11-oz can),
    drained, seeded and chopped
½ teaspoon ground cumin
½ teaspoon dried oregano leaves
1 can (11 oz) whole kernel corn with
    red and green peppers, drained
⅛ teaspoon paprika
⅓ cup sliced green onions
1 small tomato, cut into 6 wedges

1 Heat oven to 400°F. In 10-inch skillet, cook beef and onion over medium-high heat 9 to 10 minutes, stirring frequently, until beef is thoroughly cooked; drain.

2 Meanwhile, in 2-quart saucepan, mix water, butter and salt. Heat to boiling. Remove from heat. Stir in milk and potato flakes. Cover; let stand 5 minutes. Stir in green chiles and ½ cup of the cheese.

3 To beef mixture, add enchilada sauce, chipotle chiles, cumin and oregano; mix well. Heat to boiling. Remove from heat. Spread beef mixture in ungreased shallow 2-quart casserole. Top with corn. Spread potatoes evenly over corn. Sprinkle with remaining ½ cup cheese.

4 Bake 13 to 17 minutes or until cheese is melted and filling is bubbly. Sprinkle with paprika and green onions. Arrange tomato wedges in center of casserole. Let stand 5 minutes before serving.

High Altitude (3500–6500 ft): Place casserole in oven on cookie sheet with sides in case of spillover.

1 Serving: Calories 440; Total Fat 24g (Saturated Fat 12g; Trans Fat 1.5g); Cholesterol 105mg; Sodium 790mg; Total Carbohydrate 28g (Dietary Fiber 3g) **Exchanges:** 1½ Starch, 1 Vegetable, 3 Lean Meat, 2½ Fat **Carbohydrate Choices:** 2

28   Pillsbury Best of the Bake-Off® Casseroles

california casserole

10 SERVINGS

PREP TIME: *1 hour*

START TO FINISH: *1 hour 25 minutes*

MRS. HILDRETH H. HATHEWAY
Santa Barbara, CA
Bake-Off® Contest 08, 1956

1 In small bowl or food-storage plastic bag, mix ⅓ cup flour and the paprika. Add veal; coat well with flour mixture.

2 In 12-inch skillet, heat ¼ cup oil over medium-high heat. Add veal; cook until browned. Add ½ teaspoon salt, the pepper and 1 cup water. Heat to boiling. Reduce heat; simmer uncovered about 30 minutes, stirring occasionally, until veal is tender. Transfer veal mixture to ungreased 13 × 9-inch (3-quart) glass baking dish or 3-quart casserole.

3 In same skillet, mix 1 can cream of chicken soup and 1½ cups water. Heat to boiling, stirring constantly. Pour over veal mixture in baking dish. Add onions; mix well.

4 Heat oven to 425°F. In large bowl, mix 2 cups flour, the baking powder, poppy seed, minced onion, celery seed, poultry seasoning and ¼ teaspoon salt. Add ¼ cup oil and enough milk so that, when stirred, dry ingredients are just moistened.

5 In small bowl, mix melted butter and bread crumbs. Drop rounded tablespoons of dough into crumb mixture; roll to coat well. Arrange dumplings over warm veal mixture. Bake 20 to 25 minutes or until dumplings are deep golden brown.

6 Meanwhile, in 2-quart saucepan, mix sauce ingredients. Heat just to boiling. Reduce heat; simmer uncovered 2 to 3 minutes, stirring frequently, until hot. Serve sauce with casserole and dumplings.

High Altitude (3500–6500 ft): No change.

1 Serving: Calories 500; Total Fat 27g (Saturated Fat 9g; Trans Fat 0g); Cholesterol 105mg; Sodium 960mg; Total Carbohydrate 37g (Dietary Fiber 2g) **Exchanges:** 2 Starch, ½ Other Carbohydrate, 3 Lean Meat, 3 Fat **Carbohydrate Choices:** 2½

CASSEROLE

⅓ cup Pillsbury BEST all-purpose flour

1 teaspoon paprika

2 lb boneless veal, cut into 1-inch pieces

¼ cup vegetable oil

½ teaspoon salt

⅛ teaspoon pepper

1 cup water

1 can (10¾ oz) condensed cream of chicken soup

1½ cups water

1 jar (16 oz) small whole onions, drained

DUMPLINGS

2 cups Pillsbury BEST all-purpose flour

4 teaspoons baking powder

1 tablespoon poppy seed, if desired

1 teaspoon instant minced onion

1 teaspoon celery seed

1 teaspoon poultry seasoning

¼ teaspoon salt

¼ cup vegetable oil

¾ to 1 cup milk

2 tablespoons butter or margarine, melted

½ cup unseasoned dry bread crumbs

SAUCE

1 can (10¾ oz) condensed cream of chicken soup

1 container (8 oz) sour cream

¼ cup milk

tamale casserole

EVELYN HINES

St. Louis, MO

Bake-Off® Contest 36, 1994

8 SERVINGS

PREP TIME: *20 minutes*

START TO FINISH: *50 minutes*

1½ lb lean (at least 80%) ground beef

1½ teaspoons garlic powder

1½ teaspoons chili powder

1 to 1½ teaspoons seasoned salt

1 can (6 oz) tomato paste

¾ cup water

1 can (14.5 oz) cut green beans, drained

1 can (11 oz) whole kernel corn, drained

1 package (8 or 8.5 oz) corn muffin mix*

1 egg

⅔ cup milk*

12 oz prepared cheese product, cut into cubes

*If using 7- or 8-oz package corn muffin mix, make muffin mix as directed on package—except double the amount of milk.

1 Heat oven to 450°F. Grease and flour, or spray with cooking spray with flour 12 × 8-inch (2-quart) or 13 × 9-inch (3-quart) glass baking dish. In 10-inch skillet, cook beef over medium-high heat 9 to 10 minutes, stirring frequently, until thoroughly cooked; drain. Add garlic powder, chili powder, seasoned salt and tomato paste; mix well. Stir in water. Gently fold in beans and corn. Reduce heat; simmer uncovered 10 minutes, stirring occasionally.

2 Meanwhile, in small bowl, make muffin batter as directed on package, using egg and ⅔ cup milk. Spread half of muffin batter in pan. Spoon beef mixture over batter; press cubes of cheese into beef mixture. Top with remaining muffin batter.

3 Bake 20 to 25 minutes or until golden brown and set. Let stand 10 minutes; cut into squares.

High Altitude (3500–6500 ft): Heat oven to 425°F.

1 Serving: Calories 490; Total Fat 28g (Saturated Fat 14g; Trans Fat 1.5g); Cholesterol 140mg; Sodium 1510mg; Total Carbohydrate 30g (Dietary Fiber 4g) **Exchanges:** 1½ Starch, ½ Low-Fat Milk, 2 Lean Meat, 1 High-Fat Meat, 2 Fat **Carbohydrate Choices:** 2

mexican crescent bake

4 SERVINGS

PREP TIME: *20 minutes*

START TO FINISH: *45 minutes*

MRS. SUZANNE L. SISSON
Palatine, IL
Bake-Off® Contest 27, 1976

1 Heat oven to 375°F.

2 In 10-inch skillet, cook beef, onion and seasoning mix over medium heat 8 to 10 minutes, stirring occasionally, until beef is thoroughly cooked; drain. Stir in refried beans. Separate dough into 2 rectangles. Place in ungreased 13 × 9-inch pan; press over bottom and ½ inch up sides to form crust. Firmly press perforations to seal.

3 Spoon meat mixture over crust; sprinkle with olives. In medium bowl, mix sour cream and egg; stir in cheese. Spoon sour cream mixture over meat. (No need to spread.) Bake 25 to 30 minutes or until edges of crust are golden brown. Serve immediately.

High Altitude (3500–6500 ft): No change.

1 lb lean (at least 80%) ground beef

¼ cup chopped onion or 1 tablespoon instant minced onion

1 package (1.31 oz) sloppy joe seasoning mix

1 can (16 oz) refried beans or pork and beans, undrained

1 can (8 oz) Pillsbury refrigerated crescent dinner rolls

⅓ cup sliced pimiento-stuffed green olives

1 cup sour cream

1 egg

2 cups shredded Cheddar cheese (8 oz)

1 Serving: Calories 920; Total Fat 59g (Saturated Fat 29g; Trans Fat 4.5g); Cholesterol 230mg; Sodium 2010mg; Total Carbohydrate 50g (Dietary Fiber 6g) **Exchanges:** 3 Starch, 5½ High-Fat Meat, 2½ Fat **Carbohydrate Choices:** 3

easy-to-make crescent barbecue bake

MISS MONICA STAVISH
McKees Rocks, PA
Bake-Off® Contest 24, 1973

5 SERVINGS
PREP TIME: *15 minutes*
START TO FINISH: *30 minutes*

1 lb lean (at least 80%) ground beef

¼ cup chopped onion or 1 tablespoon instant minced onion

½ to 1 cup barbecue sauce

1 can (8 oz) Pillsbury refrigerated crescent dinner rolls

1 cup shredded Cheddar cheese (4 oz)

1 Heat oven to 375°F.

2 In 10-inch skillet, cook beef and onion over medium heat 8 to 10 minutes, stirring occasionally, until beef is thoroughly cooked; drain. Stir in barbecue sauce. Reduce heat; simmer uncovered, stirring occasionally, while preparing crust. Separate dough into 2 large rectangles. Place in ungreased 13 × 9-inch pan; press over bottom and 1 inch up sides to form crust. Firmly press perforations to seal. Spread hot meat mixture over dough; sprinkle with cheese.

3 Bake 15 to 20 minutes or until edges of crust are golden brown.

High Altitude (3500–6500 ft): No change.

1 Serving: Calories 460; Total Fat 27g (Saturated Fat 12g; Trans Fat 3.5g); Cholesterol 80mg; Sodium 800mg; Total Carbohydrate 29g (Dietary Fiber 0g) **Exchanges:** 2 Starch, 3 High-Fat Meat **Carbohydrate Choices:** 2

crescent cheeseburger bake

MRS. C. B. WHITTEN
Salem, IL
Bake-Off® Contest 22, 1971

4 SERVINGS
PREP TIME: *20 minutes*
START TO FINISH: *45 minutes*

1 to 1¼ lb lean (at least 80%)
  ground beef
¼ cup chopped onion or 1 tablespoon
  instant minced onion
1 clove garlic, finely chopped,
  or ½ teaspoon garlic salt
2 cups shredded Swiss, Cheddar
  or American cheese (8 oz)
1 teaspoon salt
½ teaspoon paprika
⅛ teaspoon pepper
1 teaspoon lemon juice
½ teaspoon Worcestershire sauce
1 egg
1 can (8 oz) Pillsbury refrigerated
  crescent dinner rolls

1 Heat oven to 375°F. In 10-inch skillet, cook beef, onion and garlic over medium heat 8 to 10 minutes, stirring occasionally, until beef is thoroughly cooked; drain. Remove from heat. Stir in remaining ingredients except crescents; set aside.

2 Separate dough into 4 rectangles. In ungreased 11 × 7-inch glass baking dish or 9- or 8-inch square pan, press 4 rectangles. Press over bottom and ½ inch up sides to form crust. Spoon meat mixture into crust.*

3 Bake 25 to 30 minutes or until crust is golden brown.

*To make ahead, prepare, cover and refrigerate up to 2 hours before baking. Bake as directed.

High Altitude (3500–6500 ft): No change.

1 Serving: Calories 640; Total Fat 41g (Saturated Fat 19g; Trans Fat 4g); Cholesterol 175mg; Sodium 1210mg; Total Carbohydrate 27g (Dietary Fiber 0g) **Exchanges:** 1½ Starch, 3 Lean Meat, 2 High-Fat Meat, 3 Fat **Carbohydrate Choices:** 2

hearty crescent beef bake

4 SERVINGS
PREP TIME: *15 minutes*
START TO FINISH: *45 minutes*

MRS. VYRLA KAY JACKSON
South Bend, IN
Bake-Off® Contest 22, 1971

1 Heat oven to at 350°F. In 10-inch skillet, cook beef and onions over medium heat 8 to 10 minutes, stirring occasionally, until beef is thoroughly cooked and onions are tender; drain. Stir in mushrooms, salt and pepper; set aside.

2 Separate dough into 8 triangles. In ungreased 9-inch glass pie plate or 8- or 9-inch square pan, place triangles. Press over bottom and up sides to form crust. Spoon beef mixture into crust. In small bowl, mix sour cream and eggs. Pour sour cream mixture over meat; sprinkle with paprika.

3 Bake 30 to 35 minutes or until topping is set and crust is golden brown.

High Altitude (3500–6500 ft): In step 1, stir 2 tablespoons flour in with mushrooms. In step 2, use 9-inch square pan. In step 3, bake 45 to 50 minutes.

1 to 1¼ lb lean (at least 80%) ground beef

2 medium onions, sliced thin and separated into rings

2 jars (4.5 oz each) sliced mushrooms, drained

1½ teaspoons salt

¼ to ½ teaspoon pepper

1 can (8 oz) Pillsbury refrigerated crescent dinner rolls

1 cup sour cream

2 eggs

Paprika

1 Serving: Calories 590; Total Fat 39g (Saturated Fat 17g; Trans Fat 4.5g); Cholesterol 215mg; Sodium 1590mg; Total Carbohydrate 31g (Dietary Fiber 2g) **Exchanges:** 1½ Starch, 1½ Vegetable, 3 Lean Meat, 5½ Fat **Carbohydrate Choices:** 2

spinach beef crescent bake

MRS. PATRICIA DEMILLE
Elmont, NY
Bake-Off® Contest 27, 1976

4 SERVINGS
PREP TIME: *20 minutes*
START TO FINISH: *55 minutes*

1 can (8 oz) Pillsbury refrigerated crescent dinner rolls

1 lb lean (at least 80%) ground beef

1 can (4 oz) mushroom pieces and stems, drained

1 cup shredded Swiss or Cheddar cheese (4 oz)

¼ cup thinly sliced green onion or 1 tablespoon instant minced onion

1 box (9 oz) frozen spinach* or cut broccoli, thawed, well-drained

4 eggs

¼ cup grated Parmesan cheese

1 teaspoon salt

¼ teaspoon pepper

½ cup milk

*1 lb fresh spinach, cooked, may be substituted for the frozen spinach.

1 Heat oven to 350°F. Separate dough into 4 rectangles. In ungreased 12 × 8-inch (2-quart) glass baking dish or shallow 2-quart casserole, place rectangles. Press over bottom and ½ inch up sides to form crust.

2 In 10-inch skillet, cook beef over medium heat 8 to 10 minutes, stirring occasionally, until thoroughly cooked; drain. Stir in mushrooms, shredded cheese and onion; heat until hot.

3 Spoon hot beef mixture evenly over dough. Press spinach between paper towels to remove all moisture; arrange well-drained spinach over meat mixture. In small bowl, beat eggs with whisk or fork; stir in remaining ingredients. Pour egg mixture over spinach.

4 Bake 32 to 36 minutes or until crust is deep golden brown and filling is firm. Cool 10 minutes; cut into squares to serve.

High Altitude (3500–6500 ft): No change.

1 Serving: Calories 660; Total Fat 40g (Saturated Fat 17g; Trans Fat 4g); Cholesterol 315mg; Sodium 1460mg; Total Carbohydrate 30g (Dietary Fiber 3g) **Exchanges:** 1½ Starch, 1 Vegetable, 5 High-Fat Meat **Carbohydrate Choices:** 2

chuckwagon crescent casserole

5 SERVINGS

PREP TIME: *20 minutes*

START TO FINISH: *55 minutes*

MRS. SALLY CAPPON
Satellite Beach, FL
Bake-Off® Contest 23, 1972

1 Heat oven to 350°F. In 10-inch skillet, cook beef and onion over medium heat 8 to 10 minutes, stirring occasionally, until beef is thoroughly cooked; drain. Stir in soup, enchilada sauce, garlic salt and pepper. Heat to boiling. Reduce heat; simmer uncovered, stirring occasionally, while preparing crust.

2 Separate dough into 2 large rectangles. In ungreased 12 × 8-inch (2-quart) or 13 × 9-inch (3-quart) glass baking dish, place rectangles. Press over bottom and 1½ inches up sides to form crust. Firmly press perforations to seal. Sprinkle ¾ cup of the corn chips over crust. Spoon beef mixture over corn chips. Sprinkle with cheese and remaining ¾ cup corn chips. Pour milk over casserole. Sprinkle with parsley and paprika.

3 Bake 25 to 30 minutes or until crust is golden brown. Let stand 5 minutes before cutting.

High Altitude (3500–6500 ft): No change.

1 lb lean (at least 80%) ground beef
½ cup chopped onion or 2 tablespoons instant minced onion
1 can (10¾ oz) condensed cream of mushroom soup
1 can (10 oz) mild enchilada sauce
½ teaspoon garlic salt
⅛ teaspoon pepper
1 can (8 oz) Pillsburyrefrigerated crescent dinner rolls
1½ cups crushed corn chips
1 cup shredded Cheddar cheese (4 oz)
½ cup milk
Parsley flakes
Paprika

1 Serving: Calories 660; Total Fat 41g (Saturated Fat 14g; Trans Fat 3.5g); Cholesterol 85mg; Sodium 1560mg; Total Carbohydrate 43g (Dietary Fiber 2g) **Exchanges:** 2½ Starch, ½ Other Carbohydrate, 2 Lean Meat, 1 High-Fat Meat, 5 Fat **Carbohydrate Choices:** 3

golden layers biscuit taco casserole

LOUISE V. DAVIS
Oakley, MI
Bake-Off® Contest 37, 1996

8 SERVINGS
PREP TIME: *30 minutes*
START TO FINISH: *40 minutes*

1 jar (16 oz) taco sauce

1 can (12 oz) Pillsbury Grands! Jr. Golden Layers refrigerated biscuits

1 cup shredded sharp Cheddar cheese (4 oz)

1 cup shredded mozzarella cheese (4 oz)

1 can (2.25 oz) sliced ripe olives, drained

½ lb lean (at least 80%) ground beef

¼ cup chopped red bell pepper, if desired

¼ cup chopped green bell pepper, if desired

1 can (4 oz) mushroom pieces and stems, drained, if desired

1 Heat oven to 400°F. Lightly spray 13 × 9-inch (3-quart) glass baking dish with cooking spray. Spread taco sauce evenly in bottom of dish.

2 Separate dough into 10 biscuits. Cut each biscuit into quarters. Place biscuit pieces in taco sauce; turn to coat. Sprinkle ½ cup of the Cheddar cheese, ½ cup of the mozzarella cheese and the olives over top; stir gently to mix.

3 Bake 15 to 18 minutes or until bubbly. Meanwhile, in 8-inch skillet, cook beef, bell peppers and mushrooms over medium-high heat 5 to 7 minutes, stirring frequently, until beef is thoroughly cooked; drain.

4 Remove baking dish from oven. Sprinkle remaining ½ cup Cheddar cheese and ½ cup mozzarella cheese over mixture. Top evenly with beef mixture.

5 Bake 5 to 7 minutes longer or until mixture bubbles vigorously around edges.

High Altitude (3500–6500 ft): Increase bake time in step 3 to 18 to 21 minutes.

1 Serving: Calories 310; Total Fat 17g (Saturated Fat 7g; Trans Fat 2.5g); Cholesterol 40mg; Sodium 1030mg; Total Carbohydrate 22g (Dietary Fiber 1g) **Exchanges:** 1½ Starch, 1½ Medium-Fat Meat, 1½ Fat **Carbohydrate Choices:** 1½

pizza crescent casserole

MRS. LINDA CARREL
Romulus, MI
Bake-Off® Contest 23, 1972

4 SERVINGS
PREP TIME: *20 minutes*
START TO FINISH: *45 minutes*

1 to 1½ lb lean (at least 80%) ground beef

¼ cup chopped onion or 1 tablespoon instant minced onion

¼ cup chopped green bell pepper

¼ cup grated Parmesan cheese

½ teaspoon salt

Dash pepper

3 slices bacon, crisply cooked, crumbled

2 cans (8 oz each) Pillsbury refrigerated crescent dinner rolls

1 can (8 oz) pizza sauce

½ cup shredded mozzarella cheese (2 oz)

1 Heat oven to 375°F. In 10-inch skillet, cook beef, onion and green pepper over medium heat 8 to 10 minutes, stirring occasionally, until beef is thoroughly cooked; drain. Stir in Parmesan cheese, salt, pepper and bacon.

2 Meanwhile, separate each can dough into 4 rectangles. On work surface, firmly press perforations to seal. Spread 2 to 3 tablespoons beef mixture on each rectangle (reserve remaining mixture). Starting at shorter side, roll up each rectangle. Place rolls in ungreased 8- or 9-inch square pan.

3 Stir pizza sauce into remaining beef mixture in saucepan. Heat to boiling. Reduce heat; simmer uncovered, stirring occasionally, 2 minutes. Pour evenly over rolls. Sprinkle with mozzarella cheese.

4 Bake 25 to 35 minutes or until golden brown and rolls are no longer doughy.

High Altitude (3500–6500 ft): In step 3, do not sprinkle with cheese. In step 4, bake 30 to 40 minutes, adding cheese during last 5 minutes of bake time.

1 Serving: Calories 750; Total Fat 44g (Saturated Fat 17g; Trans Fat 7g); Cholesterol 90mg; Sodium 1640mg; Total Carbohydrate 51g (Dietary Fiber 1g) **Exchanges:** 3½ Starch, 3 Lean Meat, 1 High-Fat Meat, 4½ Fat **Carbohydrate Choices:** 3½

pop-up pizza casserole

PREP TIME: *20 minutes*
START TO FINISH: *45 minutes*

SHIRLIE M. BYAM (MRS. BEN)
Lynnwood, WA
Bake-Off® Contest 29, 1980

1 Heat oven to 400°F. In 10-inch skillet, cook beef over medium heat 9 to 11 minutes, stirring occasionally, until thoroughly cooked; drain. Stir in onions, bell pepper, garlic, oregano, salt, water, pepper sauce, tomato sauce and sauce mix. Heat to boiling. Reduce heat; simmer uncovered, stirring occasionally, 10 minutes.

2 Meanwhile, in small bowl, beat milk, oil and eggs with electric mixer at medium speed 1 minute. Add flour and salt; beat about 2 minutes or until smooth. Pour hot meat mixture into ungreased 13 × 9-inch pan; top with cheese slices. Pour batter over cheese, covering filling completely. Sprinkle with Parmesan cheese.

3 Bake 25 to 30 minutes or until puffed and deep golden brown. Serve immediately.

High Altitude (3500–6500 ft): No change.

CASSEROLE

- 1½ lb lean (at least 80%) ground beef
- 1 cup chopped onions or ¼ cup dried chopped onion
- 1 cup chopped green bell pepper or ¼ cup sweet pepper flakes
- 1 clove garlic, finely chopped, or ⅛ teaspoon dried minced garlic
- ½ teaspoon dried or ground oregano leaves
- Dash salt
- ½ cup water
- ⅛ teaspoon red pepper sauce
- 1 can (15 oz) tomato sauce
- 1 package (1.5 oz) spaghetti sauce mix
- 6 to 8 oz sliced mozzarella, provolone or Monterey Jack cheese

POPOVER BATTER

- 1 cup milk
- 1 tablespoon vegetable oil
- 2 eggs
- 1 cup Pillsbury BEST all-purpose or unbleached flour
- ½ teaspoon salt
- ½ cup grated Parmesan cheese

1 Serving: Calories 310; Total Fat 16g (Saturated Fat 7g; Trans Fat 0.5g); Cholesterol 100mg; Sodium 920mg; Total Carbohydrate 19g (Dietary Fiber 1g) **Exchanges:** 1 Starch, 3 Medium-Fat Meat **Carbohydrate Choices:** 1

cheese steak crescent braids

CINDY JOY

Alameda, CA

Bake-Off® Contest 33, 1988

6 SERVINGS

PREP TIME: *35 minutes*

START TO FINISH: *1 hour*

1 tablespoon butter or margarine

4 portions thinly sliced frozen sandwich steaks (from 12.25-oz box), cut crosswise into ½-inch strips

1 large green bell pepper, cut into thin bite-sized strips (1½ cups)

1 medium onion, chopped (½ cup)

2 cans (8 oz each) Pillsbury refrigerated crescent dinner rolls

1 cup shredded mozzarella cheese (4 oz)

1 egg, beaten, if desired

1 Heat oven to 350°F. In 10-inch skillet, melt butter over medium-high heat. Add steak strips; cook 8 to 10 minutes, stirring frequently, until no longer pink. Remove steak from skillet; place on plate. Add bell pepper and onion to skillet; cook about 5 minutes, stirring occasionally, or until crisp-tender. Return cooked steak to skillet; mix well. Add salt and pepper to taste.

2 On ungreased cookie sheet, unroll 1 can of dough Firmly press perforations and edges to seal. Press or roll into 13 × 7-inch rectangle.

3 Spoon heaping cup of steak mixture in 2-inch-wide strip lengthwise down center of dough to within ¼ inch of each end. Sprinkle ½ cup of the cheese over steak mixture.

4 Make cuts 1 inch apart on long sides of rectangle just to edge of filling. For braided appearance, fold strips of dough at an angle halfway across filling with ends slightly overlapping, alternating from side to side. Fold ends of braid under to seal. On second ungreased cookie sheet, repeat with remaining can of dough, steak mixture and cheese. Brush braids with beaten egg.

5 Bake 16 to 22 minutes or until golden brown, switching position of cookie sheets in oven halfway through baking. Cool 1 minute; remove braids from cookie sheets. Let stand 5 minutes before serving. Cut into slices.

High Altitude (3500–6500 ft): No change.

1 **Serving:** Calories 410; Total Fat 23g (Saturated Fat 9g; Trans Fat 4g); Cholesterol 35mg; Sodium 710mg; Total Carbohydrate 32g (Dietary Fiber 1g) **Exchanges:** 1½ Starch, ½ Other Carbohydrate, 2 Medium-Fat Meat, 2½ Fat **Carbohydrate Choices:** 2

grands! roast beef sandwiches

CANDACE BARNHART
Hollywood, CA
Bake-Off® Contest 39, 2000

8 SANDWICHES

PREP TIME: *15 minutes*
START TO FINISH: *40 minutes*

SANDWICHES

1 can (16.3 oz) Pillsbury Grands!
refrigerated buttermilk biscuits

2 tablespoons butter or margarine,
melted

¼ cup garlic herb dry bread crumbs

⅓ cup mayonnaise or salad dressing

1 can (4.5 oz) chopped green chiles

8 slices (1 oz each) cooked roast beef
(from deli)

1 cup finely shredded Monterey Jack
cheese (4 oz)

SAUCE, IF DESIRED

½ cup mayonnaise or salad dressing

¼ cup Dijon mustard

1 Heat oven to 375°F. Separate dough into 8 biscuits. Brush tops and sides of biscuits with melted butter; coat with bread crumbs. On ungreased cookie sheet, place biscuits 2 inches apart, crumb side up. Sprinkle any remaining bread crumbs over biscuits.

2 Bake 14 to 16 minutes or until golden brown. Cool 5 minutes. Set oven control to broil.

3 Meanwhile, in small bowl, stir together ⅓ cup mayonnaise and the green chiles. Split biscuits; place tops and bottoms, cut sides up, on same cookie sheet. Spread mayonnaise mixture evenly on top halves of biscuits. Arrange roast beef slices on bottom halves, folding to fit. Sprinkle with cheese.

4 Broil 4 to 6 inches from heat 2 to 3 minutes or until cheese is melted and mayonnaise mixture is bubbly. Place top halves of biscuits over bottom halves. In small bowl, stir together sauce ingredients. Serve with sandwiches.

High Altitude (3500–6500 ft): No change.

1 Sandwich: Calories 400; Total Fat 26g (Saturated Fat 10g; Trans Fat 3.5g); Cholesterol 40mg; Sodium 1070mg; Total Carbohydrate 28g (Dietary Fiber 0g) **Exchanges:** 1½ Starch, ½ Other Carbohydrate, 1½ Medium-Fat Meat, 3 Fat **Carbohydrate Choices:** 2

italian meatball hoagie braids

BEVERLEY ROSSELL
Morgantown, IN
Bake-Off® Contest 39, 2000

8 SANDWICHES

PREP TIME: *15 minutes*
START TO FINISH: *35 minutes*

2 cans (8 oz each) Pillsbury refrigerated crescent dinner rolls or 2 cans (8 oz each) Pillsbury Crescent Recipe Creations™ refrigerated flaky dough sheet

16 frozen cooked Italian-style meatballs, 1 to 1½ inch (from 16-oz bag), thawed, halved

1 cup tomato-basil pasta sauce

1 cup shredded mozzarella cheese (4 oz)

1 egg, slightly beaten

¼ cup grated Parmesan cheese

1 Heat oven to 375°F. Spray 2 cookie sheets with cooking spray.

2 If using crescent rolls: Unroll dough; separate into 8 rectangles. Place rectangles on cookie sheets. Firmly press perforations to seal. If using dough sheet: Unroll dough; cut into 8 rectangles. Place rectangles on cookie sheets.

3 Place 4 meatball halves lengthwise down center of each rectangle. Top each rectangle with 2 tablespoons pasta sauce and 2 tablespoons mozzarella cheese. With scissors or sharp knife, make cuts 1 inch apart on long sides of dough to within ½ inch of filling. Alternately cross strips over filling. Brush dough with beaten egg; sprinkle with Parmesan cheese.

4 Bake 15 to 20 minutes or until golden brown.

High Altitude (3500–6500 ft): Bake 18 to 23 minutes.

1 Sandwich: Calories 450; Total Fat 25g (Saturated Fat 10g; Trans Fat 3.5g); Cholesterol 95mg; Sodium 1040mg; Total Carbohydrate 35g (Dietary Fiber 1g) **Exchanges:** 2 Starch, ½ Other Carbohydrate, 2 High-Fat Meat, 1½ Fat **Carbohydrate Choices:** 2

neat-to-eat sloppy joe crescents

RHODA SCHRAG
Ritzville, WA
Bake-Off® Contest 24, 1973

4 SANDWICHES

PREP TIME: *15 minutes*
START TO FINISH: *35 minutes*

¾ lb lean (at least 80%) ground beef

½ cup ketchup

¼ cup chopped onion

1 tablespoon yellow mustard

2 teaspoons Worcestershire sauce

⅛ teaspoon pepper

½ cup shredded Cheddar cheese (2 oz)

1 can (8 oz) Pillsbury refrigerated crescent dinner rolls

Sesame seed, if desired

1 Heat oven to 375°F. In 10-inch skillet, cook beef over medium-high heat 5 to 7 minutes, stirring frequently, until thoroughly cooked; drain. Stir in ketchup, onion, mustard, Worcestershire sauce, pepper and cheese. Remove from heat.

2 Separate dough into 4 rectangles. On work surface, firmly press perforations to seal. Press each rectangle into a 5-inch square. Spoon about ½ cup of the meat mixture onto center of each square. Fold dough over to make triangle; seal edges with fork. Place triangles on ungreased cookie sheet. Cut 1 to 2 slits in top of each triangle. Sprinkle with sesame seed.

3 Bake 14 to 20 minutes or until golden brown.

High Altitude (3500–6500 ft): No change.

1 Sandwich: Calories 460; Total Fat 26g (Saturated Fat 11g; Trans Fat 4g); Cholesterol 70mg; Sodium 970mg; Total Carbohydrate 32g (Dietary Fiber 1g) **Exchanges:** 1 Starch, 1 Other Carbohydrate, 3 Medium-Fat Meat, 2 Fat **Carbohydrate Choices:** 2

toasted mexi-meatball hoagies

JENNY FLAKE
Gilbert, AZ
Bake-Off® Contest 42, 2006

4 SERVINGS
PREP TIME: *45 minutes*
START TO FINISH: *1 hour 15 minutes*

ROLLS
2 cans (11 oz each) Pillsbury
  refrigerated crusty French loaf

MEATBALLS
2 tablespoons extra-virgin olive oil
1 package (1 oz) taco seasoning mix
1 egg, slightly beaten
1 lb lean (at least 80%) ground beef
½ cup garlic herb bread crumbs
½ cup chopped fresh cilantro
½ cup finely chopped onion
½ teaspoon finely chopped garlic
¼ teaspoon freshly ground
  black pepper
2 tablespoons chunky-style salsa
1 teaspoon red pepper sauce

SAUCE
1¼ cups ranch dressing
¼ cup chopped fresh cilantro
¼ cup chunky-style salsa
1 tablespoon fresh lime juice

TOPPINGS
2 cups shredded iceberg lettuce
1 cup shredded Cheddar cheese
  (4 oz)
1 cup diced tomatoes (2 small)
¼ cup chopped fresh cilantro

1 Heat oven to 350°F. Grease or spray large cookie sheet. Remove dough from both cans; place seam side down and 3 inches apart on cookie sheet. Cut 4 or 5 diagonal slashes (½-inch deep) with sharp knife on top of each loaf. Bake 26 to 30 minutes or until deep golden brown. Cool slightly while making meatballs, about 25 minutes.

2 Spread oil in bottom of 13 × 9-inch (3-quart) glass baking dish. Measure out 1 teaspoon of the taco seasoning mix for sauce; set aside. In large bowl, place remaining seasoning mix. Add remaining meatball ingredients; mix well. Shape mixture into 1-inch balls; place in baking dish. Bake uncovered 25 to 30 minutes, turning meatballs once halfway through baking, until no longer pink in center.

3 Meanwhile, in food processor, place remaining taco seasoning mix and sauce ingredients. Cover; process until smooth. Set aside.

4 Set oven control to broil. Cut each loaf in half horizontally, cutting to— but not completely through—one long side. Place cut side up on cookie sheet. Broil with top 5 to 6 inches from heat 1 to 2 minutes or just until lightly toasted.

5 Spread ¼ cup sauce on each toasted cut side. Spoon hot meatballs evenly onto bottom halves of loaves. Top evenly with toppings. Drizzle with remaining sauce. If desired, close sandwiches. Cut each sandwich in half. Serve immediately.

High Altitude (3500–6500 ft): No change.

1 Serving (½ Sandwich): Calories 1240; Total Fat 73g (Saturated Fat 20g; Trans Fat 1g); Cholesterol 175mg; Sodium 3040mg; Total Carbohydrate 102g (Dietary Fiber 2g) **Exchanges:** 5½ Starch, 1½ Other Carbohydrate, 4 Medium-Fat Meat, 10 Fat **Carbohydrate Choices:** 7

Reuben in the Round Crescents (page 72) ▶

franks and beans casserole

MRS. WILLIAM VAUGHAN
Richmond, VA
Bake-Off® Contest 28, 1978

6 SERVINGS

PREP TIME: *15 minutes*
START TO FINISH: *55 minutes*

CASSEROLE

3 tablespoons packed brown sugar

1 teaspoon ground mustard

3 tablespoons ketchup

1 can (21 oz) pork and beans, undrained

1 can (15 oz) chili without beans

1 lb hot dogs, sliced

1 can (2.8 oz) French-fried onions

TOPPING

1¼ cups instant mashed potato flakes

1 cup Pillsbury BEST all-purpose or unbleached flour*

1½ teaspoons baking powder

½ teaspoon salt

¾ cup milk

2 tablespoons butter or margarine, melted

1 can (8.5 oz) cream-style corn

1 egg

1 tablespoon parsley flakes

*If using Pillsbury BEST self-rising flour, omit baking powder and salt.

1 Heat oven to 400°F. In ungreased 3-quart casserole or 13 × 9-inch (3-quart) glass baking dish, mix all casserole ingredients.

2 In medium bowl, mix all topping ingredients except parsley flakes. Drop by spoonfuls around edge of casserole; sprinkle with parsley flakes.

3 Bake 35 to 40 minutes or until topping is light golden brown and meat mixture is bubbly.

High Altitude (3500–6500 ft): In step 1, add 3 tablespoons water to bean mixture.

1 Serving: Calories 740; Total Fat 41g (Saturated Fat 15g; Trans Fat 3g); Cholesterol 110mg; Sodium 2360mg; Total Carbohydrate 69g (Dietary Fiber 8g) **Exchanges:** 2½ Starch, 2 Other Carbohydrate, 2 High-Fat Meat, 4½ Fat **Carbohydrate Choices:** 4½

ham 'n yam biscuit bake

6 SERVINGS
PREP TIME: *20 minutes*
START TO FINISH: *40 minutes*

MRS. SHIRLEY A. DESANTIS
Bethlehem, PA
Bake-Off® Contest 28, 1978

1 Heat oven to 375°F.

2 In 10-inch ovenproof skillet, melt butter. Stir in brown sugar and ¼ cup syrup; heat until bubbly. Add 1 cup ham, ½ cup peanuts and the sweet potatoes, stirring gently to blend. Reduce heat; simmer uncovered, stirring occasionally, while preparing biscuits.

3 Separate dough into 10 biscuits. On work surface, press or roll each biscuit into a 3-inch round. Place 1-inch ham cube in center of eachround. Fold dough over ham, covering completely; seal well.* Arrange filled biscuits on hot sweet potato mixture. Brush or drizzle with 2 tablespoons syrup; sprinkle with ¼ cup peanuts.

4 Bake 20 to 25 minutes or until deep golden brown. Serve hot.

*If you don't have an ovenproof skillet, pour hot ham mixture into ungreased 12 X 8-inch glass baking dish or shallow 3-quart casserole. Top with biscuits and bake as directed.

High Altitude (3500–6500 ft): Bake 25 to 30 minutes.

CASSEROLE
¼ cup butter or margarine
¼ cup packed brown sugar
¼ cup maple-flavored syrup
1 cup cubed cooked ham (4 oz)
½ cup chopped peanuts, if desired
1 can (17 oz) vacuum-pack sweet potatoes, drained, whole or sliced (about 3 cups)

TOPPING
1 can (12 oz) Pillsbury Grands! Jr. Golden Layers refrigerated biscuits
10 (1-inch) cubes cooked ham
2 tablespoons maple-flavored syrup
¼ cup chopped peanuts

1 Serving: Calories 550; Total Fat 26g (Saturated Fat 10g; Trans Fat 3g); Cholesterol 50mg; Sodium 1180mg; Total Carbohydrate 64g (Dietary Fiber 2g) **Exchanges:** 1 Starch, 3 Other Carbohydrate, 2 Lean Meat, 4 Fat **Carbohydrate Choices:** 4

frank 'n bean biscuit casserole

DENNIS BATICH
Garwood, NJ
Bake-Off® Contest 23, 1972

8 SERVINGS
PREP TIME: *20 minutes*
START TO FINISH: *45 minutes*

2 tablespoons butter or margarine

½ cup chopped onion or 2 tablespoons dried minced onion

¾ cup chopped green bell pepper

1 lb hot dogs, sliced

⅓ cup chili sauce

⅓ cup ketchup

1 to 2 tablespoons packed brown sugar, if desired

1 can (15 oz) baked beans or pork and beans, undrained

1 can (7.5 oz) Pillsbury refrigerated buttermilk or Country biscuits

¾ cup shredded Cheddar cheese (3 oz)

1 cup corn chips, crushed

3 tablespoons grated Romano or Parmesan cheese

1 Heat oven to 375°F. In 10-inch skillet, melt 1 tablespoon of the butter over medium-high heat. Add onion and bell pepper; cook and stir until tender.

2 Add hot dogs, chili sauce, ketchup, brown sugar and beans; stir gently to mix. Reduce heat; simmer uncovered 2 minutes, stirring occasionally. Spoon hot mixture into ungreased 11 × 7- or 12 × 8-inch (2-quart) glass baking dish.

3 Separate dough into 10 biscuits. Separate each biscuit into 2 layers. Arrange 10 biscuit layers over hot beef mixture. Sprinkle with Cheddar cheese. Arrange remaining biscuit layers on top to cover.

4 In small bowl, mix corn chips and Romano cheese. Sprinkle over biscuits. Dot with remaining tablespoon butter.

5 Bake 20 to 25 minutes or until biscuits are golden brown.

High Altitude (3500–6500 ft): Bake 25 to 30 minutes.

1 Serving: Calories 470; Total Fat 29g (Saturated Fat 11g; Trans Fat 0.5g); Cholesterol 55mg; Sodium 1600mg; Total Carbohydrate 37g (Dietary Fiber 5g) **Exchanges:** 2 Starch, 1½ High-Fat Meat, 3½ Fat **Carbohydrate Choices:** 2½

baked pork chops with biscuit stuffin'

MRS. MARION OHL
Clyde, OH
Bake-Off® Contest 22, 1971

6 SERVINGS

PREP TIME: *20 minutes*
START TO FINISH: *1 hour 15 minutes*

1 tablespoon vegetable oil

6 pork loin chops, ½ inch thick

1 can (10¾ oz) condensed cream of
  chicken soup

1 cup chopped celery

1 cup chopped onions

1 egg

¼ teaspoon pepper

⅛ teaspoon poultry seasoning

1 can (7.5 oz) Pillsbury refrigerated
  buttermilk or Country biscuits

1 Heat oven to 350°F. In 10-inch skillet, heat oil over medium heat until hot. Add pork chops; cook until browned on both sides. In ungreased 13 × 9-inch pan, place pork chops.

2 In medium bowl, mix soup, celery, onions, egg, pepper and poultry seasoning.

3 Separate dough into 10 biscuits Cut each biscuit into 8 pieces. Stir biscuit pieces into soup mixture. Spoon over pork chops.

4 Bake 45 to 55 minutes or until biscuit pieces are golden brown and no longer doughy in center.

High Altitude (3500–6500 ft): In step 1, use medium-high heat. In step 4, bake 50 to 55 minutes.

1 Serving: Calories 560; Total Fat 23g (Saturated Fat 6g; Trans Fat 0g); Cholesterol 110mg; Sodium 1380mg; Total Carbohydrate 56g (Dietary Fiber 2g) **Exchanges:** 1½ Starch, 2 Other Carbohydrate, 4 Medium-Fat Meat **Carbohydrate Choices:** 4

ham and spinach potato casserole

8 SERVINGS

PREP TIME: *20 minutes*
START TO FINISH: *1 hour 15 minutes*

JILL COX
Sioux City, IA
Bake-Off® Contest 34, 1990

1 Heat oven to 350°F. Grease or spray 13 × 9-inch (3-quart) glass baking dish. In 4-quart saucepan, heat water, butter and salt to a rolling boil. Remove from heat. Stir in milk and potato flakes with fork until potatoes are desired consistency; set aside.

2 In medium bowl, mix onion, pepper, spinach, sour cream, cream cheese and eggs. Spread mixture in baking dish. Sprinkle ham over spinach mixture. Top with hot mashed potatoes. Cover with foil.

3 Bake 35 to 40 minutes or until mixture just begins to bubble at edges. Remove foil; sprinkle Cheddar cheese evenly over top. Bake uncovered 3 to 5 minutes longer or until cheese is melted. Let stand 10 minutes before serving.

High Altitude (3500–6500 ft): No change.

2⅔ cups water
¼ cup butter or margarine
1 teaspoon salt, if desired
1 cup milk
2⅔ cups mashed potato flakes
¼ cup finely chopped onion
⅛ teaspoon pepper
1 box (9 oz) frozen spinach, thawed, well drained
1 container (8 oz) sour cream
1 package (3 oz) cream cheese, softened
2 eggs
3 cups cubed cooked ham
1 cup shredded Cheddar cheese (4 oz)

1 Serving: Calories 420; Total Fat 29g (Saturated Fat 16g; Trans Fat 0.5g); Cholesterol 145mg; Sodium 710mg; Total Carbohydrate 18g (Dietary Fiber 2g) **Exchanges:** 1 Starch, 2½ Medium-Fat Meat, 3 Fat **Carbohydrate Choices:** 1

crafty crescent lasagna

BETTY TAYLOR
Dallas, TX
Bake-Off® Contest 19, 1968

8 SERVINGS
PREP TIME: *30 minutes*
START TO FINISH: *1 hour*

MEAT FILLING

½ lb pork sausage
½ lb lean (at least 80%) ground beef
¾ cup chopped onions
1 tablespoon parsley flakes
½ teaspoon dried basil leaves
½ teaspoon dried oregano leaves
1 small clove garlic, finely chopped
Dash pepper
1 can (6 oz) tomato paste

CHEESE FILLING

¼ cup grated Parmesan cheese
1 cup cottage cheese
1 egg

CRUST

2 cans (8 oz each) Pillsbury
    refrigerated crescent dinner rolls
2 (7 × 4-inch) slices mozzarella cheese
1 tablespoon milk
1 tablespoon sesame seed

1 Heat oven to 375°F. In 10-inch skillet, cook sausage and beef over medium-high heat, stirring frequently, until thoroughly cooked and no longer pink; drain. Stir in remaining meat filling ingredients; cook about 5 minutes, stirring occasionally, until hot.

2 In small bowl, mix cheese filling ingredients. Unroll both cans of dough into 2 large rectangles. On ungreased cookie sheet, place rectangles with long sides together. Firmly press edges and perforations to seal. Press to form 15 × 13-inch rectangle.

3 Spoon half of meat filling in 6-inch-wide strip lengthwise down center of dough to within 1 inch of short sides. Spoon cheese filling over meat filling; spoon remaining meat filling evenly over cheese filling. Arrange mozzarella cheese slices over meat mixture.

4 Fold shortest sides of dough 1 inch over filling. Fold long sides of dough tightly over filling, overlapping edges in center ¼ inch. Firmly pinch center seam and ends to seal. Brush with milk; sprinkle with sesame seed.

5 Bake 23 to 27 minutes or until deep golden brown.

High Altitude (3500–6500 ft): No change.

1 Serving: Calories 410; Total Fat 24g (Saturated Fat 9g; Trans Fat 3.5g); Cholesterol 65mg; Sodium 930mg; Total Carbohydrate 29g (Dietary Fiber 1g) **Exchanges:** 1 Starch, ½ Other Carbohydrate, 2½ Medium-Fat Meat, 2½ Fat **Carbohydrate Choices:** 2

asparagus ham crescent bake

MRS. GENEVA RADER
Raleigh, NC
Bake-Off® Contest 27, 1976

4 SERVINGS
PREP TIME: *20 minutes*
START TO FINISH: *50 minutes*

1 can (8 oz) Pillsbury refrigerated
crescent dinner rolls

1¼ cups frozen asparagus cuts,
cooked drained, or 1 can (10.5 oz)
cut asparagus spears, well drained

1 cup cubed cooked ham (4 oz)

3 eggs

½ cup half-and-half or milk

1 to 1½ cups shredded American or
Swiss cheese (4 to 6 oz)

1 can (2.8 oz) French-fried onions

1 Heat oven to 350°F.

2 Separate dough into 2 rectangles. In ungreased 13 × 9-inch pan or 12-inch pizza pan, place rectangles. Press over bottom and ½ inch up sides to form crust. Firmly press perforations to seal. Arrange asparagus and ham over dough. Beat eggs with whisk or fork; blend in half-and-half. Pour over ham; sprinkle with cheese.*

3 Bake 25 minutes. Sprinkle with French-fried onions. Bake 5 to 10 minutes longer or until crust is deep golden brown.

*To make ahead, prepare, cover and refrigerate up to 2 hours; bake as directed.

High Altitude (3500–6500 ft): No change.

1 Serving: Calories 700; Total Fat 49g (Saturated Fat 20g; Trans Fat 6g); Cholesterol 235mg; Sodium 1460mg; Total Carbohydrate 34g (Dietary Fiber 1g) **Exchanges:** 2 Starch, ½ Vegetable, 3½ Medium-Fat Meat, 5 Fat **Carbohydrate Choices:** 2

swiss and corn crescent bake

6 SERVINGS

PREP TIME: *20 minutes*

START TO FINISH: *55 minutes*

MRS. JOHN W. SISSON (SUZANNE)

Palatine, IL

Bake-Off® Contest 28, 1978

1 Heat oven to 375°F.

2 Separate dough into 2 long rectangles. In ungreased 13 × 9-inch pan, place rectangles. Press over bottom and ½ inch up sides to form crust. Firmly press perforations to seal. Sprinkle onions and bacon over crust.

3 In medium bowl, mix eggs and sour cream; stir in cheese and corn. Spoon cheese mixture evenly over bacon.*

4 Bake 25 to 30 minutes or until filling is set and crust is deep golden brown. Cool 5 minutes. Cut into squares to serve.

*To make ahead, prepare, cover and refrigerate up to 2 hours; bake as directed.

High Altitude (3500–6500 ft): No change.

1 can (8 oz) Pillsbury refrigerated crescent dinner rolls

1 can (2.8 oz) French-fried onion rings

½ lb (8 slices) bacon, crisply cooked, crumbled

2 eggs, slightly beaten

1 cup sour cream

2 cups shredded Swiss or Cheddar cheese (8 oz)

1 can (8.5 oz) cream-style corn

1 Serving: Calories 570; Total Fat 40g (Saturated Fat 18g; Trans Fat 4.5g); Cholesterol 140mg; Sodium 870mg; Total Carbohydrate 30g (Dietary Fiber 0g) **Exchanges:** 1½ Starch, ½ Other Carbohydrate, 2½ Medium-Fat Meat, 5½ Fat **Carbohydrate Choices:** 2

ham 'n cheese omelet bake

JULIE AMBERSON
Browns Point, WA
Bake-Off® Contest 41, 2004

8 SERVINGS

PREP TIME: *15 minutes*
START TO FINISH: *1 hour 15 minutes*

1 box (10 oz) frozen cut broccoli in a cheese flavored sauce

1 can (10.2 oz) Pillsbury Grands! Flaky Layers refrigerated original biscuits (5 biscuits)

10 eggs

1½ cups milk

1 teaspoon ground mustard

Salt and pepper, if desired

2 cups diced cooked ham

⅓ cup chopped onion

1 cup shredded Cheddar cheese (4 oz)

1 cup shredded Swiss cheese (4 oz)

1 jar (4.5 oz) sliced mushrooms, drained

1 Heat oven to 350°F. Cut small slit in center of broccoli and cheese sauce pouch. Microwave on High 3 to 4 minutes, rotating pouch ¼ turn once halfway through microwaving. Set aside to cool slightly.

2 Meanwhile, spray bottom only of 13 × 9-inch (3-quart) glass baking dish with cooking spray. Separate dough into 5 biscuits. Cut each biscuit into 8 pieces. Arrange evenly in baking dish.

3 In large bowl, beat eggs, milk, mustard, salt and pepper with wire whisk until well blended. Stir in ham, onion, both cheeses, mushrooms and cooked broccoli and cheese sauce. Pour mixture over biscuit pieces in baking dish. Press down with back of spoon, making sure all biscuit pieces are covered with egg mixture.

4 Bake 40 to 50 minutes or until edges are deep golden brown and center is set. Let stand 10 minutes before serving. Cut into squares.

High Altitude (3500–6500 ft): Heat oven to 375°F.

1 Serving: Calories 450; Total Fat 28g (Saturated Fat 11g; Trans Fat 2.5g); Cholesterol 315mg; Sodium 1090mg; Total Carbohydrate 22g (Dietary Fiber 1g) **Exchanges:** 1½ Starch, 3½ Medium-Fat Meat, 1½ Fat **Carbohydrate Choices:** 1½

bean and sausage bake

MARJORIE FORTIER
West Redding, CT
Bake-Off® Contest 35, 1992

8 SERVINGS
PREP TIME: *15 minutes*
START TO FINISH: *40 minutes*

CASEROLE

- ¾ lb bulk hot Italian sausage
- ½ cup coarsely chopped onion
- ½ cup coarsely chopped green bell pepper
- ½ cup coarsely chopped red bell pepper
- 1 tablespoon finely chopped garlic
- ¾ cup ketchup
- 3 teaspoons chili powder
- 1 tablespoon chopped fresh or 2 teaspoons dried cilantro leaves, crushed
- ¾ teaspoon ground cumin
- 1 can (16 oz) baked beans, undrained
- 1 can (15 oz) black beans, drained, rinsed
- 1 can (15 oz) garbanzo beans, drained
- 1 can (11 oz) whole kernel corn, drained

TOPPINGS, AS DESIRED

- 1 to 2 cups shredded Monterey Jack cheese (4 to 8 oz)
- 1 to 1½ cups sour cream
- Crushed red pepper flakes

1 Heat oven to 375°F.

2 In 10-inch skillet, cook sausage with onion, bell peppers and garlic over medium-high heat until sausage is no longer pink and vegetables are crisp-tender; drain. Stir in ketchup, chili powder, cilantro and cumin; mix well.

3 In ungreased 13 × 9-inch (3-quart) glass baking dish, mix baked beans, black beans, garbanzo beans and corn. Spoon sausage mixture over beans. DO NOT STIR.

4 Bake 25 to 30 minutes or until bubbly and hot. Remove from oven; stir well. Serve with toppings.

High Altitude (3500–6500 ft): No change.

1 Serving (1 Cup Without Toppings): Calories 510; Total Fat 21g (Saturated Fat 9g; Trans Fat 0g); Cholesterol 50mg; Sodium 1280mg; Total Carbohydrate 56g (Dietary Fiber 12g) **Exchanges:** 2 Starch, 1½ Other Carbohydrate, 1 Vegetable, 2 Lean Meat, 2½ Fat **Carbohydrate Choices:** 4

sausage crescent braid

5 SERVINGS

PREP TIME: *15 minutes*

START TO FINISH: *40 minutes*

JONI ETHERINGTON

Leawood, KS

Bake-Off® Contest 41, 2004

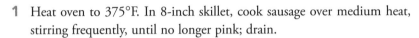

1 Heat oven to 375°F. In 8-inch skillet, cook sausage over medium heat, stirring frequently, until no longer pink; drain.

2 In large bowl, mix spinach, cottage cheese, Parmesan cheese, garlic and cooked sausage.

3 If using crescent rolls: Unroll dough into 1 large rectangle on ungreased cookie sheet. Press into 13 × 8-inch rectangle. Firmly press perforations and edges to seal. If using dough sheet: Unroll dough on ungreased cookie sheet. Press into 13 × 8-inch rectangle.

4 Spoon sausage mixture in 4-inch-wide strip lengthwise down center of rectangle. Top with slices of both cheeses.

5 With scissors or sharp knife, make cuts 1 inch apart on long sides of dough rectangle to within ½ inch of sausage mixture. Fold strips of dough up over sausage mixture to meet in center; pinch to seal.

6 Bake 18 to 24 minutes or until golden brown. Remove from cookie sheet; cut into crosswise slices. Serve warm.

High Altitude (3500–6500 ft): No change.

½ lb bulk Italian turkey sausage

1 box (9 oz) frozen spinach, thawed, squeezed to drain

1 cup fat-free cottage cheese, drained

½ cup grated Parmesan cheese

1 teaspoon minced garlic in water (from 4.5-oz jar)

1 can (8 oz) Pillsbury refrigerated crescent dinner rolls or 1 can (8 oz) Pillsbury Crescent Recipe Creations refrigerated flaky dough sheet

3 slices (1 oz each) provolone cheese

3 slices (1 oz each) mozzarella cheese

1 Serving: Calories 450; Total Fat 25g (Saturated Fat 11g; Trans Fat 3g); Cholesterol 70mg; Sodium 1250mg; Total Carbohydrate 23g (Dietary Fiber 1g) **Exchanges:** 1 Starch, ½ Other Carbohydrate, 4 Medium-Fat Meat, 1 Fat **Carbohydrate Choices:** 1½

tex-mex breakfast bake

LYNNE MILLIRON
Austin, TX
Bake-Off® Contest 41, 2004

6 SERVINGS

PREP TIME: *20 minutes*
START TO FINISH: *1 hour 15 minutes*

¼ lb bulk lean breakfast sausage

1 can (10 oz) red enchilada sauce

½ cup crumbled queso fresco (Mexican cheese) or farmer cheese (2 oz)

⅓ cup sour cream

¼ cup chopped green onions (4 tablespoons)

1 can (16.3 oz) Pillsbury Grands! Flaky Layers refrigerated original or buttermilk biscuits

1¼ cups shredded Colby–Monterey Jack cheese blend (5 oz)

¼ cup chopped fresh cilantro

1 Heat oven to 350°F. Spray 8-inch square or 11 × 7-inch (2-quart) glass baking dish with cooking spray. In 10-inch skillet, cook sausage over medium-high heat, stirring frequently, until no longer pink.

2 Meanwhile, in small bowl, mix ¼ cup of the enchilada sauce, the queso fresco, sour cream and onions; set aside. Pour remaining enchilada sauce into medium bowl. Separate dough into 8 biscuits. Cut each biscuit into 8 pieces. Gently stir dough pieces into enchilada sauce to coat. Spoon mixture into baking dish; spread evenly.

3 Drain sausage on paper towels. Sprinkle sausage evenly on top of biscuit pieces. Spread sour cream mixture evenly over sausage.

4 Bake 30 to 35 minutes or until center is set and edges are deep golden brown. Sprinkle with Colby–Monterey Jack cheese

5 Bake about 10 minutes longer or until cheese is bubbly. Sprinkle with cilantro. Garnish with tomato slices, if desired. Let stand 5 minutes before serving. Cut into squares.

High Altitude (3500–6500 ft): In step 1, heat oven to 375°F. Use 11 × 7-inch (2-quart) glass baking dish. In step 4, bake 45 to 50 minutes. Sprinkle with Colby–Monterey Jack cheese. In step 5, bake about 5 minutes longer.

1 Serving: Calories 450; Total Fat 27g (Saturated Fat 10g; Trans Fat 4.5g); Cholesterol 40mg; Sodium 1370mg; Total Carbohydrate 37g (Dietary Fiber 1g) **Exchanges:** 2 Starch, 1 Other Carbohydrate, 1 High-Fat Meat, 3 Fat **Carbohydrate Choices:** 2½

ham and swiss crescent braid

LORRAINE MAGGIO
Manlius, NY
Bake-Off® Contest 39, 2000

8 SERVINGS
PREP TIME: *15 minutes*
START TO FINISH: *55 minutes*

¾ lb cooked ham, chopped (2¼ cups)

1 cup frozen broccoli florets, thawed

1 cup shredded Swiss cheese (4 oz)

1 jar (4.5 oz) sliced mushrooms, drained

½ cup mayonnaise or salad dressing

1 tablespoon honey mustard

2 cans (8 oz each) Pillsbury refrigerated crescent dinner rolls* or 2 cans (8 oz each) Pillsbury Crescent Recipe Creations refrigerated flaky dough sheet

1 egg white, beaten

2 tablespoons slivered almonds

*If using Pillsbury Big & Flaky large refrigerated crescent dinner rolls, make as directed—except form into 16 × 14-inch rectangle.

1 Heat oven to 375°F. Spray cookie sheet with cooking spray. In large bowl, mix ham, broccoli, cheese, mushrooms, mayonnaise and mustard.

2 If using crescent rolls: Unroll both cans of dough into 2 large rectangles. Place dough with long sides together on cookie sheet, forming 15 × 12-inch rectangle. Firmly press perforations and edges to seal. If using dough sheets: Unroll both cans of dough into 2 large rectangles. Place dough with long sides together on cookie sheet, forming 15 × 12-inch rectangle. Firmly press edges to seal.

3 Spoon and spread ham mixture lengthwise in 6-inch-wide strip down center of dough. With scissors or sharp knife, make cuts 1½ inches apart on long sides of dough to within ½ inch of filling. Twisting each strip once, alternately cross strips over filling. Tuck short ends under; press to seal. Brush dough with beaten egg white. Sprinkle with almonds.

4 Bake 28 to 33 minutes or until deep golden brown. Cool 5 minutes. Cut crosswise into slices.

High Altitude (over 3500 ft): Not recommended.

1 Serving: Calories 460; Total Fat 31g (Saturated Fat 10g; Trans Fat 3g); Cholesterol 45mg; Sodium 1260mg; Total Carbohydrate 25g (Dietary Fiber 1g) **Exchanges:** 1½ Starch, 2 Medium-Fat Meat, 4 Fat **Carbohydrate Choices:** 1½

swiss ham ring-around

MRS. LYMAN FRANCIS
Cheshire, CT
Bake-Off® Contest 20, 1969

8 SERVINGS

PREP TIME: *20 minutes*
START TO FINISH: *50 minutes*

1 tablespoon butter or margarine, softened

¼ cup chopped fresh parsley or 2 tablespoons dried parsley flakes

2 tablespoons finely chopped onion or 1½ teaspoons dried minced onion

2 tablespoons yellow mustard

1 teaspoon lemon juice

1½ cups shredded Swiss cheese (6 oz)

1 cup chopped fresh broccoli or frozen chopped broccoli, cooked, drained

1 cup diced cooked ham

1 can (8 oz) Pillsbury refrigerated crescent dinner rolls

1 Heat oven to 350°F. Grease or spray large cookie sheet. In large bowl, mix butter, parsley, onion, mustard and lemon juice. Add cheese, cooked broccoli and ham; mix lightly. Set aside.

2 Separate dough into 8 triangles. Arrange triangles on cookie sheet with shortest sides toward center, overlapping in wreath shape and leaving a 3-inch round opening in center.

3 Spoon ham filling on widest part of dough. Pull end points of triangles over filling and tuck under dough to form a ring.

4 Bake 25 to 30 minutes or until golden brown.

High Altitude (3500–6500 ft): In step 1, stir 2 tablespoons Pillsbury BEST all-purpose flour into ham and cheese mixture.

1 Serving: Calories 240; Total Fat 15g (Saturated Fat 7g; Trans Fat 1.5g); Cholesterol 35mg; Sodium 570mg; Total Carbohydrate 14g (Dietary Fiber 0g) **Exchanges:** 1 Starch, 1½ Medium-Fat Meat, 1 Fat **Carbohydrate Choices:** 1

reuben in the round crescents

MRS. IRENE DUNN
Cuyahoga Falls, OH
Bake-Off® Contest 27, 1976

8 SERVINGS
PREP TIME: *25 minutes*
START TO FINISH: *50 minutes*

2 cans (8 oz each) Pillsbury refrigerated crescent dinner rolls

1 package (8 oz) thinly sliced pastrami or corned beef

1 package (6 oz) Swiss or mozzarella cheese (4 slices)

1 can (8 oz) sauerkraut, drained

½ teaspoon caraway seed

½ teaspoon sesame seed

1 Heat oven to 400°F. Separate 1 can of dough into 4 rectangles. Place in rectangles in ungreased 12-inch pizza pan or 13 × 9-inch pan. Press over bottom and ½ inch up sides to form crust. Firmly press perforations to seal.

2 Layer pastrami, cheese and sauerkraut over dough; sprinkle with caraway seed. Separate second can of dough into 8 triangles. With points toward center, arrange triangles in spoke pattern over filling (do not seal outer edges of triangles to bottom crust). Sprinkle with sesame seed.

3 Bake 15 to 25 minutes or until golden brown. Cut into wedges or squares.

High Altitude (3500–6500 ft): No change.

Photo on page 51.

1 Serving: Calories 340; Total Fat 20g (Saturated Fat 8g; Trans Fat 3g); Cholesterol 30mg; Sodium 1050mg; Total Carbohydrate 25g (Dietary Fiber 1g) **Exchanges:** 1½ Starch, 1½ High-Fat Meat, 1½ Fat **Carbohydrate Choices:** 1½

broccoli brunch braid

8 SERVINGS

PREP TIME: *25 minutes*

START TO FINISH: *1 hour*

DIANE TUCKER

Blackfoot, ID

Bake-Off® Contest 33, 1988

1 In 10-inch skillet, cook sausage over medium-high heat 8 to 10 minutes, stirring occasionally, until no longer pink; drain; set aside. Cook broccoli as directed on package. Drain; set aside.

2 Heat oven to 325°F. In large bowl, mix 1 beaten egg, flour and baking powder; beat well with spoon. Stir in cheeses, mushrooms, cooked sausage and broccoli.

3 If using crescent rolls: Unroll dough; separate into 2 long rectangles. Place on ungreased large cookie sheet, with long sides overlapping ½ inch. Firmly press perforations and edges to seal. Press or roll to form 14 × 10-inch rectangle. If using dough sheet: Unroll dough; cut into 2 long rectangles. Place on ungreased large cookie sheet, with long sides overlapping ½ inch. Press or roll to form 14 × 10-inch rectangle.

4 Spoon sausage mixture in 3½-inch-wide strip lengthwise down center of rectangle to within ¼ inch of each end. Form sausage mixture into mounded shape. Make cuts 1 inch apart on long sides of rectangle just to edge of filling. For braided appearance, fold strips of dough at an angle halfway across filling with ends slightly overlapping, alternating from side to side. Brush with beaten egg white; sprinkle with caraway seed.

5 Bake 25 to 35 minutes or until deep golden brown. Cool 5 minutes; remove from cookie sheet. Cut into slices.

High Altitude (3500–6500 ft): Heat oven to 350°F. Bake 30 to 37 minutes.

½ lb bulk pork sausage

2 cups frozen cut broccoli

1 egg, beaten

1 tablespoon Pillsbury BEST all-purpose flour

¼ teaspoon baking powder

½ cup ricotta cheese

1 cup shredded Cheddar cheese (4 oz)

1 jar (4.5 oz) sliced mushrooms, drained

1 can (8 oz) Pillsbury refrigerated crescent dinner rolls or 1 can (8 oz) Pillsbury Crescent Recipe Creations refrigerated flaky dough sheet

1 egg white, beaten

¼ teaspoon caraway seed

1 Serving: Calories 260; Total Fat 16g (Saturated Fat 7g; Trans Fat 1.5g); Cholesterol 55mg; Sodium 520mg; Total Carbohydrate 15g (Dietary Fiber 1g) **Exchanges:** 1 Starch, 1½ High-Fat Meat, ½ Fat **Carbohydrate Choices:** 1

quick corn and mushroom brunch squares

HELEN HUBER
Conroe, TX
Bake-Off® Contest 33, 1988

12 SERVINGS
PREP TIME: *20 minutes*
START TO FINISH: *1 hour*

2 cans (8 oz each) Pillsbury refrigerated crescent dinner rolls

2 cups chopped cooked ham

1½ cups shredded Monterey Jack cheese (6 oz)

1½ cups shredded Swiss cheese (6 oz)

1 can (11 oz) whole kernel corn with red and green peppers, drained

1 jar (4.5 oz) sliced mushrooms, drained

6 eggs

1 cup milk

½ teaspoon salt, if desired

¼ to ½ teaspoon pepper

1 Heat oven to 375°F. Unroll both cans of dough into 4 long rectangles. Place crosswise in ungreased 15 × 10 × 1-inch pan. Press firmly over bottom and ¾ inch up sides to form crust. Firmly press perforations and edges to seal.

2 Sprinkle ham, cheeses, corn and mushrooms evenly over crust. In medium bowl, beat eggs with whisk or fork, milk, salt and pepper until well blended. Pour evenly over ham, cheeses and vegetables.

3 Bake 35 to 40 minutes or until crust is deep golden brown, egg mixture is set and knife inserted in center comes out clean. Cool 5 minutes. Cut into squares.

High Altitude (3500–6500 ft): Bake 37 to 42 minutes.

1 Serving: Calories 360; Total Fat 22g (Saturated Fat 10g; Trans Fat 2g); Cholesterol 145mg; Sodium 900mg; Total Carbohydrate 22g (Dietary Fiber 0g) **Exchanges:** 1½ Starch, 2 Medium-Fat Meat, 2 Fat **Carbohydrate Choices:** 1½

Maryland Chicken Supper (page 76) ▶

maryland chicken supper

TERESA HUESTIS

Wheaton, MD

Bake-Off® Contest 16, 1964

6 SERVINGS

PREP TIME: *30 minutes*

START TO FINISH: *1 hour 10 minutes*

CHICKEN MIXTURE

¾ cup chopped onions

½ cup chopped celery

1 tablespoon chopped green onion tops, if desired

¼ cup chicken broth

1 can (10½ oz) cream of chicken soup

1 cup sour cream

3 cups cubed cooked chicken

1 can (4 oz) sliced mushrooms, drained

3 slices bacon, crisply cooked, crumbled, if desired

1 teaspoon salt

1 teaspoon Worcestershire sauce

⅛ teaspoon pepper

CONFETTI BISCUITS

1 cup Pillsbury BEST all-purpose flour*

2 teaspoons baking powder

½ teaspoon salt

2 eggs, slightly beaten

½ cup milk

1 tablespoon finely chopped green bell pepper

1 tablespoon finely chopped red bell pepper or chopped pimientos, drained (from 2-oz jar)

1 cup shredded Cheddar cheese (4 oz)

TOPPING

¼ cup shredded Cheddar cheese (1 oz)

*If using Pillsbury BEST self-rising flour, omit baking powder and salt in biscuits.

1 Heat oven to 350°F. In 1-quart saucepan over medium-high heat, heat onions, celery, green onions and chicken broth to boiling. Reduce heat; simmer covered 20 minutes, stirring occasionally. In ungreased 2-quart casserole, mix onion mixture, soup, sour cream, chicken, mushrooms, bacon, salt, Worcestershire sauce and pepper.

2 In medium bowl, mix flour, baking powder and ½ teaspoon salt. Add eggs, milk, bell peppers and 1 cup cheese; mix just until blended. Drop biscuits by tablespoonfuls onto casserole.

3 Bake 40 to 45 minutes or until golden brown. Sprinkle with ¼ cup cheese. Bake 2 to 5 minutes longer or until cheese begins to melt.

High Altitude (3500–6500 ft): Increase first bake time to 55 to 60 minutes.

Photo on page 75.

1 Serving: Calories 470; Total Fat 26g (Saturated Fat 13g; Trans Fat 1g); Cholesterol 185mg; Sodium 1460mg; Total Carbohydrate 27g (Dietary Fiber 1g) **Exchanges:** 1½ Starch, 1 Vegetable, 3½ Lean Meat, 3 Fat **Carbohydrate Choices:** 2

chicken cheese enchiladas

6 SERVINGS
PREP TIME: *15 minutes*
START TO FINISH: *40 minutes*

BARBIE LEE
Tavernier, FL
Bake-Off® Contest 40, 2002

1 Heat oven to 350°F. In resealable food-storage plastic bag, mix taco seasoning mix, oil and ¼ cup of the water; seal bag and mix well. Add chicken pieces; turn to mix. Refrigerate 5 minutes or up to 12 hours.

2 In medium bowl, mix 2½ cups of the Monterey Jack cheese, the cilantro, salt, ricotta cheese, chiles and egg.

3 Heat 10-inch nonstick skillet over medium-high heat until hot. Add chicken with marinade; cook and stir 5 to 10 minutes or until chicken is no longer pink in center.

4 In ungreased 13 × 9-inch (3-quart) glass baking dish, mix ½ cup of the salsa and remaining ¼ cup water. Spread evenly in bottom of baking dish. Spoon ⅓ cup cheese mixture down center of each tortilla. Top with chicken; roll up. Place filled tortillas, seam side down, over salsa mixture in baking dish. Drizzle enchiladas with remaining salsa. Sprinkle with remaining ½ cup Monterey Jack cheese.

5 Bake 20 to 25 minutes or until cheese is melted.

High Altitude (3500–6500 ft): Heat oven to 375°F. Bake 25 to 30 minutes. Cover with foil during last 10 to 15 minutes of bake time if tortillas begin to dry out.

1 package (1 oz) taco seasoning mix

1 tablespoon olive oil

½ cup water

1 lb boneless skinless chicken breasts, cut into bite-size pieces or strips

3 cups shredded Monterey Jack cheese (12 oz)

⅓ cup chopped fresh cilantro

½ teaspoon salt

1 container (15 oz) ricotta cheese

1 can (4.5 oz) chopped green chiles

1 egg

1 jar (16 oz) chunky-style salsa

12 flour tortillas for soft tacos and fajitas (from two 8.2-oz packages)

1 Serving (2 Enchiladas): Calories 730; Total Fat 31g (Saturated Fat 14g; Trans Fat 1.5g); Cholesterol 140mg; Sodium 2200mg; Total Carbohydrate 62g (Dietary Fiber 4g) **Exchanges:** 2½ Starch, 2 Other Carbohydrate, 5 Medium-Fat Meat, 1 Fat **Carbohydrate Choices:** 4

fiesta chicken empanada

JANIELLE FISHER
Newark, DE
Bake-Off® Contest 39, 2000

6 SERVINGS

PREP TIME: *15 minutes*
START TO FINISH: *40 minutes*

CRUST
1 box (15 oz) Pillsbury refrigerated pie
  crusts, softened as directed on box

FILLING
1 tablespoon olive oil

1 medium onion, sliced

½ medium red bell pepper, cut into
  2 × ¼-inch strips

½ medium green bell pepper, cut into
  2 × ¼-inch strips

½ medium yellow bell pepper, cut into
  2 × ¼-inch strips

1 can (10 oz) chunk white chicken
  breast in water, drained

4 teaspoons dried fajita seasoning

½ cup cheese and salsa dip (from
  15-oz jar)

1 egg, beaten

TOPPINGS, AS DESIRED
Sour cream, if desired

Additional cheese and salsa dip,
  if desired

1 Heat oven to 425°F. Unroll 1 pie crust onto ungreased 14-inch pizza pan or cookie sheet.

2 In 10-inch skillet, heat oil over medium-high heat. Add onion and bell peppers; cook 5 minutes, stirring occasionally, until tender. Stir in chicken and fajita seasoning.

3 Spoon chicken mixture evenly into crust-lined pan to within 1 inch of edge. Spread ½ cup dip over chicken mixture. Brush edge of crust with water. Unroll second crust; place over filling, pressing edge firmly to seal. Brush top with beaten egg.

4 Bake 20 to 25 minutes or until deep golden brown, covering edge of crust with strips of foil after 10 to 15 minutes of baking to prevent excessive browning. Cut into wedges; serve with sour cream and dip.

High Altitude (3500–6500 ft): Bake 25 to 30 minutes.

1 Serving: Calories 420; Total Fat 24g (Saturated Fat 8g; Trans Fat 0g); Cholesterol 65mg; Sodium 1000mg; Total Carbohydrate 41g (Dietary Fiber 1g) **Exchanges:** 2½ Starch, ½ Vegetable, 4½ Fat **Carbohydrate Choices:** 3

chicken manicotti olé

5 SERVINGS

PREP TIME: *30 minutes*

START TO FINISH: *1 hour 20 minutes*

RENEÉ MCWILLIAMS
Lincoln, NE
Bake-Off® Contest 40, 2002

1 Heat oven to 350°F. Spray 13 × 9-inch (3-quart) glass baking dish with cooking spray. Cook manicotti to desired doneness as directed on package. Drain; rinse with cold water.

2 In large bowl, mix chicken, ¾ cup of the salsa, ¾ cup of the beans, the garlic powder and pepper. In small bowl, mix remaining salsa and beans. Cover; reserve for topping.

3 Stuff manicotti with chicken mixture. Arrange in baking dish.

4 Cover with foil; bake 30 minutes. Uncover; top with reserved salsa mixture and cheese. Bake uncovered 15 to 20 minutes longer or until chicken is thoroughly cooked and cheese is melted.

High Altitude (3500–6500 ft): In step 4, after covering with foil, bake 40 minutes. Uncover; top with reserved salsa mixture and cheese. Bake uncovered 5 to 10 minutes.

10 uncooked manicotti

1 lb ground chicken or ground turkey breast

1 jar (16 oz) chunky-style salsa

1 can (15 oz) black beans, drained, rinsed

¼ teaspoon garlic powder

¼ teaspoon pepper

1 cup shredded Colby–Monterey Jack cheese blend (4 oz)

1 Serving: Calories 110; Total Fat 5g (Saturated Fat 2.5g; Trans Fat 0g); Cholesterol 15mg; Sodium 75mg; Total Carbohydrate 15g (Dietary Fiber 1g) **Exchanges:** ½ Starch, ½ Other Carbohydrate, 1 Fat **Carbohydrate Choices:** 1

speedy layered chicken enchilada pie

KAREN HALL
Minneapolis, MN
Bake-Off® Contest 40, 2002

6 SERVINGS

PREP TIME: *25 minutes*
START TO FINISH: *1 hour 10 minutes*

1 package (11 oz) flour tortillas for burritos (8 tortillas)

2 cups cubed cooked chicken

½ cup uncooked instant white rice

2 cups shredded reduced-fat Monterey Jack cheese (8 oz)

1 can (15 oz) black beans, drained, rinsed

1 can (19 oz) hot enchilada sauce

1 cup frozen shoepeg white corn, thawed

1 cup chunky-style salsa

2 tablespoons thinly sliced green onions (2 medium)

Reduced-fat sour cream, if desired

Chopped green onions, if desired

1 Heat oven to 350°F. Spray 9-inch round (2-quart) glass baking dish or casserole with cooking spray. Cut 5 of the tortillas in half. Cut remaining tortillas into 2½-inch-wide strips.

2 In large bowl, mix chicken, rice, 1 cup of the cheese, the beans and 1 cup of the enchilada sauce.

3 Layer 4 tortilla halves in bottom of baking dish. Top with ¼ cup enchilada sauce and half of the chicken mixture. Top with 2 tortilla halves; fill in empty spaces with 3 tortilla strips. Spoon corn over tortillas. Spread salsa over corn. Layer with 2 tortilla halves and 3 strips. Top with remaining half of chicken mixture. Continue layering with remaining 2 tortilla halves and strips, enchilada sauce, cheese and 2 tablespoons green onions.

4 Bake 35 to 45 minutes or until mixture is hot and cheese is melted. Cool 5 minutes. Top with sour cream and chopped green onions.

High Altitude (3500–6500 ft): In step 1, heat oven to 375°F. In step 3, do not add remaining cheese to top of casserole. In step 4, bake uncovered 40 to 50 minutes, adding cheese during last 5 minutes of bake time.

1 Serving: Calories 550; Total Fat 15g (Saturated Fat 7g; Trans Fat 1g); Cholesterol 65mg; Sodium 1760mg; Total Carbohydrate 66g (Dietary Fiber 11g) **Exchanges:** 3½ Starch, 1 Other Carbohydrate, 3 Medium-Fat Meat, ½ Fat **Carbohydrate Choices:** 4½

crunchy biscuit chicken casserole

MRS. MARTIN MILLER
Waunakee, WI
Bake-Off® Contest 27, 1976

6 SERVINGS

PREP TIME: *15 minutes*
START TO FINISH: *40 minutes*

2 cans (5 oz each) chunk chicken or 2 cups cubed cooked chicken

1 can (10¾ oz) condensed cream of chicken soup

1 can (8.25 oz) half-inch diagonal-cut green beans, drained

1 jar (2.5 oz) sliced mushrooms, undrained

1 cup shredded Cheddar or American cheese (4 oz)

½ cup mayonnaise or salad dressing

1 teaspoon lemon juice

1 can (16.3 oz) Pillsbury Grands! refrigerated buttermilk biscuits

1 to 2 tablespoons butter or margarine, melted

¼ to ½ cup crushed Cheddar cheese–flavor or seasoned croutons

1 Heat oven to 375°F. In 2-quart saucepan over medium-high heat, heat chicken, soup, green beans, mushrooms, cheese, mayonnaise and lemon juice to boiling, stirring occasionally. Into ungreased 13 × 9-inch (3-quart) glass baking dish, pour hot chicken mixture.

2 Separate dough into 8 biscuits; arrange over hot chicken mixture. Brush each biscuit with butter; sprinkle with crushed croutons.

3 Bake 23 to 27 minutes or until deep golden brown.

High Altitude (3500–6500 ft): Bake 27 to 31 minutes.

1 Serving: Calories 610; Total Fat 38g (Saturated Fat 12g; Trans Fat 3g); Cholesterol 75mg; Sodium 1580mg; Total Carbohydrate 42g (Dietary Fiber 2g) **Exchanges:** 3 Starch, 2 Medium-Fat Meat, 5 Fat **Carbohydrate Choices:** 3

chicken caliente crescent casserole

6 SERVINGS

PREP TIME: *20 minutes*

START TO FINISH: *35 minutes*

CAROL JENNINGS
Charlotte, NC
Bake-Off® Contest 31, 1984

1 Heat oven to 375°F. Separate dough into 2 long rectangles. Place in ungreased 12 × 8-inch (2-quart) glass baking dish or 13 × 9-inch pan. Press over bottom and ½ inch up sides to form crust. Firmly press perforations to seal. Sprinkle with half the corn chips.

2 Bake 10 to 12 minutes or until light golden brown.

3 Meanwhile, in 2-quart saucepan, mix soup, milk and flour until smooth; stir in chicken, onion, chiles and pimientos. Cook over medium heat, stirring frequently, until mixture comes to a boil and thickens. Pour hot chicken mixture into partially baked crust. Sprinkle with remaining corn chips and cheese. Arrange olives in diagonal rows over cheese.

4 Bake 14 to 18 minutes longer or until crust is golden brown.

High Altitude (3500–6500 ft): No change.

1 can (8 oz) Pillsbury refrigerated crescent dinner rolls

3 cups corn chips, coarsely crushed

1 can (10¾ oz) condensed cream of chicken soup

1 can (5 oz) evaporated milk

2 tablespoons Pillsbury BEST all-purpose flour

1 cup cubed cooked chicken

⅓ cup chopped onion

1 can (4 oz) chopped green chiles, drained

1 jar (2 oz) diced pimientos, drained

⅓ cup sliced ripe olives

1 Serving: Calories 530; Total Fat 30g (Saturated Fat 7g; Trans Fat 2g); Cholesterol 25mg; Sodium 1390mg; Total Carbohydrate 50g (Dietary Fiber 2g) **Exchanges:** 2 Starch, 1 Other Carbohydrate, 2½ Medium-Fat Meat, 2½ Fat **Carbohydrate Choices:** 3

chicken and black bean bake

JANET MERCER
Winter Park, FL
Bake-Off® Contest 40, 2002

8 SERVINGS
PREP TIME: *15 minutes*
START TO FINISH: *55 minutes*

CASEROLE

1 package (12 oz) bulk hot pork
  sausage

¾ cup Pillsbury BEST self-rising flour*

3 cups shredded Cheddar cheese
  (12 oz)

3 cups diced cooked chicken
  or turkey

1½ cups chunky-style salsa

1 can (15 oz) black beans, drained,
  rinsed

2 eggs

2 cans (4.5 oz each) chopped
  green chiles

TOPPINGS, AS DESIRED

Additional chunky-style salsa

Sour cream

Fresh cilantro sprigs

*Pillsbury BEST all-purpose or
unbleached flour can be substituted
for the self-rising flour. Add 1¼ teaspoons baking powder and ⅛ teaspoon
salt to flour.

1 Heat oven to 350°F. In 8-inch skillet, cook sausage over medium-high heat, stirring frequently, until no longer pink; drain.

2 In large bowl, mix sausage, flour and 1 cup of the cheese. Spread in ungreased 13 × 9-inch (3-quart) glass baking dish. Sprinkle with chicken. Top with 1½ cups salsa and the beans.

3 In medium bowl, beat eggs and chiles with whisk or fork. Stir in 1 cup of the cheese. Pour over mixture in baking dish. Sprinkle with remaining 1 cup cheese.

4 Bake 25 to 35 minutes or until set and edges are golden brown. Cool 5 minutes. Spoon onto individual serving plates. Top each serving with salsa, sour cream and cilantro.

High Altitude (over 3500 ft): Not recommended.

1 Serving: Calories 490; Total Fat 25g (Saturated Fat 12g; Trans Fat 0g); Cholesterol 160mg; Sodium 940mg; Total Carbohydrate 28g (Dietary Fiber 6g) **Exchanges:** 1½ Starch, ½ Other Carbohydrate, 4½ Medium-Fat Meat **Carbohydrate Choices:** 2

chicken suiza cornbread bake

12 SERVINGS

PREP TIME: *15 minutes*

START TO FINISH: *55 minutes*

LORI ANN NELSON
Rochester Hills, MI
Bake-Off® Contest 36, 1994

1 Heat oven to 375°F. Grease or spray 13 × 9-inch (3-quart) baking dish. In 6-inch skillet, melt butter over medium-high heat. Add onion and garlic; cook and stir 4 to 6 minutes, stirring occasionally, until tender. Set aside.

2 In large bowl, mix corn, cream-style corn, eggs and ¼ teaspoon salt. Add corn muffin mix; mix well. Fold in onion mixture. Pour into baking dish.

3 In large bowl, mix all topping ingredients except cheese. Spoon over cornbread to within 1 inch of edges. Sprinkle with cheese.

4 Bake 35 to 40 minutes or until edges are golden brown.

High Altitude (3500–6500 ft): Bake 40 to 45 minutes.

CORNBREAD

½ cup butter or margarine

1 medium onion, finely chopped (½ cup)

1 clove garlic, finely chopped

1 can (15.25 oz) whole kernel corn, drained

1 can (14.75 oz) cream-style corn

2 eggs, beaten

¼ teaspoon salt

1 box (8 or 8.5 oz) corn muffin mix

TOPPING

2½ cups cubed cooked chicken

1½ cups sour cream

2 tablespoons canned chopped mild green chiles

¼ teaspoon salt

¼ teaspoon pepper

1 can (4 oz) mushroom pieces and stems, drained

2 cups shredded Monterey Jack cheese (8 oz)

1 Serving: Calories 390; Total Fat 26g (Saturated Fat 14g; Trans Fat 1.5g); Cholesterol 130mg; Sodium 650mg; Total Carbohydrate 22g (Dietary Fiber 2g) **Exchanges:** 1½ Starch, 2 Medium-Fat Meat, 3 Fat **Carbohydrate Choices:** 1½

chicken 'n vegetable biscuit bake

MRS. NANCY EVANS
Clinton, UT
Bake-Off® Contest 22, 1971

4 SERVINGS
PREP TIME: *10 minutes*
START TO FINISH: *30 minutes*

6 slices bacon, cut into ½-inch pieces

1 can (14.5 oz) cut green beans, drained (1¾ cups), or 1 box (9 oz) frozen cut green beans, cooked and drained

1 can (10½ oz) condensed cream of chicken soup

1 to 2 cans (5 oz each) chunk chicken, undrained, or 1 cup cubed cooked chicken

1 can (7.5 oz) Pillsbury refrigerated buttermilk or Country biscuits

1 can (2.8 oz) French-fried onion rings, crushed

1 Heat oven to 350°F. In 10-inch skillet, cook bacon pieces until crisp; drain. Stir in green beans, soup and chicken. Heat to boiling. Reduce heat; simmer uncovered, stirring occasionally, while preparing biscuits.

2 Separate dough into 10 biscuits. Cut each biscuit into quarters. Spoon hot chicken mixture into ungreased 8- or 9-inch square pan or 1½-quart casserole. Sprinkle with crushed onion rings. Press biscuit quarters into crushed onion rings.

3 Bake 20 to 25 minutes or until biscuits are golden brown.

High Altitude (3500–6500 ft): Heat oven to 375°F.

1 Serving: Calories 480; Total Fat 24g (Saturated Fat 6g; Trans Fat 2.5g); Cholesterol 50mg; Sodium 1710mg; Total Carbohydrate 44g (Dietary Fiber 3g) **Exchanges:** 2½ Starch, ½ Vegetable, 1½ Lean Meat, 4 Fat **Carbohydrate Choices:** 3

savory crust chicken bake

8 SERVINGS

PREP TIME: *20 minutes*

START TO FINISH: *1 hour 5 minutes*

MRS. DOROTHY VEASEY
Fort Wayne, IN
Bake-Off® Contest 21, 1970

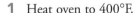

1 Heat oven to 400°F.

2 In 10-inch skillet, melt 2 tablespoons butter over medium-high heat. Cook carrot, onion and bell peppers in butter, stirring occasionally, until tender; remove from heat. Stir in chicken, soup and mushrooms; set aside.

3 In small bowl, beat ½ cup softened butter, the sour cream and egg with electric mixer at medium speed until smooth. Add flour, salt, baking powder and thyme; beat at low speed until thoroughly combined.

4 In ungreased 9-inch glass pie plate (1½ inches deep) or 12 × 8-inch (shallow 2-quart) baking dish, spread batter evenly over bottom and up sides to within 1 inch of rim. Spoon filling into crust; sprinkle with cheese.

5 Bake 25 to 30 minutes or until crust is golden brown. Let stand 10 minutes before serving. Cut in wedges; serve hot.

High Altitude (3500–6500 ft): No change.

1 Serving: Calories 420; Total Fat 30g (Saturated Fat 17g; Trans Fat 1g); Cholesterol 130mg; Sodium 930mg; Total Carbohydrate 20g (Dietary Fiber 1g) **Exchanges:** 1½ Starch, 2 Medium-Fat Meat, 3½ Fat **Carbohydrate Choices:** 1

FILLING

2 tablespoons butter or margarine

½ cup (1 medium) finely chopped carrot

½ cup (1 medium) chopped onion or 2 tablespoons dried minced onion

½ cup (1 small) chopped green bell pepper or celery

½ cup (1 small) chopped red bell pepper or 1 jar (2 oz) chopped pimientos, drained

2 cups cubed cooked chicken or turkey*

1 can (10¾ oz) condensed cream of chicken soup

1 can (4 oz) mushroom pieces and stems, drained

CRUST

½ cup butter or margarine, softened

1 cup sour cream

1 egg

1 cup Pillsbury BEST all-purpose flour**

1 teaspoon salt

1 teaspoon baking powder

½ to 1 teaspoon ground or dried thyme or sage leaves

½ to 1 cup shredded American or Cheddar cheese (2 to 4 oz)

*Three 5-oz cans chicken or turkey, drained, can be used for cooked chicken or turkey.

**If using Pillsbury BEST self-rising flour, reduce salt to ½ teaspoon, and omit baking powder.

chicken and white bean bruschetta bake

SHANNON KOHN
Simpsonville, SC
Bake-Off® Contest 42, 2006

4 SERVINGS
PREP TIME: *15 minutes*
START TO FINISH: *45 minutes*

1 can (19 oz) cannellini beans, drained, rinsed

1 can (14.5 oz) organic diced tomatoes with Italian herbs, drained

1 package (6 oz) refrigerated cooked Italian-flavor chicken breast strips, cut into 1-inch pieces

1 tablespoon balsamic vinegar

½ teaspoon salt

1 can (11 oz) Pillsbury refrigerated original breadsticks

2 cups shredded Italian cheese blend (8 oz)

½ teaspoon dried basil leaves, crushed

1 tablespoon chopped fresh parsley, if desired

1 Heat oven to 375°F. Spray 13 × 9-inch (3-quart) glass baking dish with cooking spray. In large bowl, mix beans, tomatoes, chicken, vinegar and salt.

2 Separate dough into 12 breadsticks. Cut each breadstick into 4 equal pieces. Stir ¼ of breadstick pieces at a time into bean mixture. Stir in 1 cup of the cheese. Spoon into baking dish, gently smoothing top. Top evenly with remaining 1 cup cheese; sprinkle with basil.

3 Bake 25 to 30 minutes or until bubbly and top is golden brown. To serve, spoon into individual shallow soup bowls; sprinkle with parsley.

High Altitude (3500–6500 ft): No change.

1 Serving (1½ Cups): Calories 630; Total Fat 20g (Saturated Fat 10g; Trans Fat 1g); Cholesterol 80mg; Sodium 1880mg; Total Carbohydrate 73g (Dietary Fiber 8g) **Exchanges:** 3½ Starch, 1 Other Carbohydrate, 1 Vegetable, 4 Very Lean Meat, 3 Fat **Carbohydrate Choices:** 5

stuffed poblano chile peppers

PAULA BLEVINS-RUSSELL
Alabaster, AL
Bake-Off® Contest 40, 2002

6 SERVINGS

PREP TIME: *30 minutes*
START TO FINISH: *1 hour 10 minutes*

6 poblano chiles

1 lb lean (at least 90%) ground turkey

1 package (1 oz) taco seasoning mix

1 can (15 oz) black beans, drained, rinsed

1 can (11 oz) whole kernel corn, with red and green peppers, drained

2 cups shredded light Mexican cheese blend (8 oz)

Cooking spray

1 can (14.5 oz) stewed tomatoes, undrained, chopped

1 can (4.5 oz) chopped green chiles

1 Heat oven to 350°F. Spray 13 × 9-inch (3-quart) glass baking dish with cooking spray. Cut opening in one side of each chile. Carefully remove seeds and membranes, leaving top stem intact; rinse and drain well.

2 Spray 10-inch skillet with cooking spray. Add ground turkey; cook over medium-high heat about 7 minutes, stirring frequently, until no longer pink. Add taco seasoning mix; mix well. Add beans, corn and 1 cup of the cheese; mix well. With small spoon, stuff chiles with turkey mixture. Place in baking dish. Lightly spray tops of chiles with cooking spray.

3 In small bowl, mix tomatoes and green chiles. Pour over stuffed chiles in baking dish.

4 Bake 30 to 40 minutes or until chiles are tender. Sprinkle with remaining 1 cup cheese. Bake about 3 minutes longer or until cheese is melted.

High Altitude (3500–6500 ft): Increase first bake time in step 4 to 50 to 60 minutes.

1 Serving: Calories 420; Total Fat 15g (Saturated Fat 7g; Trans Fat 0g); Cholesterol 80mg; Sodium 920mg; Total Carbohydrate 39g (Dietary Fiber 10g) **Exchanges:** 2½ Starch, 3½ Lean Meat, 1 Fat **Carbohydrate Choices:** 2½

chicken and cheese crescent chimichangas

8 SERVINGS

PREP TIME: *20 minutes*

START TO FINISH: *45 minutes*

MARLENE ZEBLECKIS
Salinas, CA
Bake-Off® Contest 33, 1988

1 Heat oven to 350°F. Grease or spray large cookie sheet. In 10-inch skillet, heat oil over medium-high heat until hot. Cook onion and garlic in oil, stirring occasionally, until onion is tender. Reduce heat to low. Add chicken; cook until hot, stirring occasionally.

2 Separate dough into 8 rectangles. Firmly press perforations to seal. Spread about 2 teaspoons of the picante on each rectangle to within ½ inch of edges. Stir 1 cup of the cheese into chicken mixture. Spoon heaping ⅓ cup chicken mixture onto half of each rectangle. Starting with short side topped with chicken, roll up; pinch ends to seal. Place seam side down on cookie sheet.

3 Bake 16 to 21 minutes or until golden brown. Remove from oven. Top each chimichanga with about 2 tablespoons of the remaining cheese. Bake 1 to 2 minutes longer or until cheese is melted. Serve with sour cream and additional picante.

High Altitude (3500–6500 ft): No change.

3 tablespoons vegetable oil

½ cup chopped onion

2 cloves garlic, finely chopped

2½ cups shredded cooked chicken

2 cans (8 oz each) Pillsbury refrigerated crescent dinner rolls

½ cup picante

2 cups shredded Cheddar cheese (8 oz)

Sour cream, as desired

Additional picante, as desired

1 Serving: Calories 490; Total Fat 32g (Saturated Fat 13g; Trans Fat 3.5g); Cholesterol 75mg; Sodium 770mg; Total Carbohydrate 26g (Dietary Fiber 0g) **Exchanges:** 1½ Starch, 3 Lean Meat, 4½ Fat **Carbohydrate Choices:** 2

peanut butter mole enchiladas

MARGARET MARTINEZ
Westminster, CO
Bake-Off® Contest 43, 2008

8 SERVINGS

PREP TIME: *20 minutes*
START TO FINISH: *50 minutes*

SAUCE

2 cans (10 oz each) mild enchilada sauce

½ cup creamy peanut butter

½ teaspoon sugar

½ teaspoon ground cinnamon

½ oz bittersweet baking chocolate

ENCHILADAS

1½ cups shredded mild white Cheddar–Monterey Jack cheese blend or Cheddar–Monterey Jack cheese blend*

1 package (11 oz) flour tortillas for burritos (8 tortillas)

2 cups cooked chicken breast strips (2¼ × ¼ inch)

¼ cup peanuts, chopped

1 teaspoon lime juice

1 container (8 oz) sour cream

2 tablespoons chopped fresh cilantro

*¾ cup shredded mild white Cheddar cheese and ¾ cup Monterey Jack cheese can be used instead of the cheese blend.

1 Heat oven to 325°F. In 2-quart saucepan, cook enchilada sauce over medium-low heat about 5 minutes, stirring occasionally, until heated. Stir in peanut butter and sugar; cook 1 to 2 minutes or until peanut butter is melted. Remove from heat. Add cinnamon and chocolate; stir until chocolate is melted.

2 Spray 13 × 9-inch (3-quart) glass baking dish with cooking spray. Spoon about ½ cup sauce over bottom of baking dish. Reserve ½ cup cheese. Fill each tortilla with about ¼ cup chicken, 2 tablespoons cheese and heaping 1 tablespoon sauce. Roll up tortillas; place seam sides down in baking dish. Pour remaining sauce evenly over tortillas.

3 Cover loosely with foil; bake 25 to 30 minutes or until thoroughly heated. Sprinkle with reserved ½ cup cheese. Bake uncovered 2 to 3 minutes longer or until cheese is melted. Sprinkle with peanuts.

4 In small bowl, stir lime juice into sour cream until mixed. Top individual servings with sour cream mixture and cilantro.

High Altitude (3500–6500 ft): Heat oven to 350°F.

1 **Serving (1 Enchilada):** Calories 500; Total Fat 31g (Saturated Fat 12g; Trans Fat 1.5g); Cholesterol 70mg; Sodium 930mg; Total Carbohydrate 31g (Dietary Fiber 1g) **Exchanges:** 1½ Starch, ½ Other Carbohydrate, 3 High-Fat Meat, 1 Fat **Carbohydrate Choices:** 2

fiesta chicken casserole

LAURENE HARSCHUTZ
Brookfield, WI
Bake-Off® Contest 32, 1986

6 SERVINGS
PREP TIME: *20 minutes*
START TO FINISH: *1 hour*

CASSEROLE

1 cup sour cream
⅓ cup milk
¼ cup chopped onion
½ teaspoon garlic salt or ¼ teaspoon garlic powder
¼ teaspoon ground cumin
Dash red pepper sauce
1 can (10¾ oz) condensed cream of chicken soup
1 box (9 oz) frozen spinach, thawed, well drained
1 can (4 oz) chopped green chiles, drained
1 jar (2 oz) chopped pimientos, drained
2 to 3 cups cubed cooked chicken
1 cup shredded Monterey Jack cheese (4 oz)
½ cup shredded Cheddar cheese (2 oz)

TOPPING

2 eggs, separated
1 cup Pillsbury BEST self-rising flour
¾ cup milk
¼ cup butter or margarine, softened
Paprika

1 Heat oven to 375°F. Lightly grease or spray with cooking spray deep 2-quart casserole. In large bowl, mix all casserole ingredients except chicken and cheeses. In medium bowl, mix chicken with cheeses. Spoon half of spinach mixture into casserole; sprinkle with half of chicken mixture. Repeat layers.

2 In small bowl, beat egg whites with electric mixer on high speed until stiff peaks form. Remove whites from bowl; set aside. In same bowl with same beaters, beat flour, ¾ cup milk, the butter and egg yolks on low speed until moistened; beat 4 minutes on high speed, scraping side of bowl occasionally. Fold in beaten egg whites. Pour topping over filling; sprinkle with paprika.

3 Bake 40 to 45 minutes or until deep golden brown.

High Altitude (3500–6500 ft): Bake 55 to 60 minutes.

1 Serving: Calories 550; Total Fat 36g (Saturated Fat 19g; Trans Fat 1g); Cholesterol 190mg; Sodium 850mg; Total Carbohydrate 28g (Dietary Fiber 2g) **Exchanges:** 2 Starch, 3 Medium-Fat Meat, 3½ Fat **Carbohydrate Choices:** 2

chicken crescent calzones

4 CALZONES

PREP TIME: *20 minutes*

START TO FINISH: *45 minutes*

MARGIE BILLINGSLEY

Austin, TX

Bake-Off® Contest 38, 1998

1 Heat oven to 375°F. Spray cookie sheet with cooking spray.

2 If using crescent rolls: Unroll dough; separate into 4 rectangles. Firmly press perforations to seal. Press each to form 6 × 5-inch rectangle. If using dough sheet: Unroll dough; cut into 4 rectangles. Press each to form a 6 × 5-inch rectangle.

3 Top each rectangle to within ½ inch of edge with slice of chicken, slice of cheese and 1 tablespoon of the mushrooms. Reserve remaining mushrooms for gravy. Fold dough in half, forming a square; pinch edges to seal. Dip each calzone in egg; coat with bread crumbs. Place on cookie sheet.

4 Bake 20 to 25 minutes or until deep golden brown.

5 Meanwhile, in 2-quart saucepan, mix gravy and reserved mushrooms. Cook over medium heat, stirring occasionally, until hot. Serve gravy over calzones. Sprinkle with onions and paprika.

High Altitude (3500–6500 ft): No change.

1 can (8 oz) Pillsbury refrigerated crescent dinner rolls* or 1 can (8 oz) Pillsbury Crescent Recipe Creations refrigerated flaky dough sheet

4 slices (2 oz each) oven-roasted chicken breast (from deli)

4 slices (1 oz each) Monterey Jack cheese

1 can (8 oz) mushroom pieces and stems, drained

1 egg, beaten

½ cup unseasoned dry bread crumbs

1 jar (12 oz) seasoned gravy for chicken

¼ cup sliced green onions (4 medium)

¼ teaspoon paprika

*If using Pillsbury Big & Flaky large refrigerated crescent dinner rolls, unroll dough and press to form 20 × 6-inch rectangle. Firmly press perforations to seal. Cut into 4 equal pieces. Continue as directed.

1 Calzone: Calories 570; Total Fat 30g (Saturated Fat 12g; Trans Fat 3.5g); Cholesterol 130mg; Sodium 1450mg; Total Carbohydrate 40g (Dietary Fiber 2g) **Exchanges:** 1½ Starch, 1 Other Carbohydrate, 4 Medium-Fat Meat, 2 Fat **Carbohydrate Choices:** 2½

rustic chicken club

SHARON KUBE
West Lafayette, IN
Bake-Off® Contest 41, 2004

6 SERVINGS
PREP TIME: *40 minutes*
START TO FINISH: *1 hour 10 minutes*

CRUST

1 Pillsbury refrigerated pie crust (from 15-oz box), softened as directed on box

FILLING

4 tablespoons mayonnaise

¾ cup shredded Monterey Jack cheese (3 oz)

2 cups chopped cooked chicken or turkey breast

1 tablespoon Dijon mustard

1 tablespoon fresh lemon juice

½ to 1 teaspoon freshly ground black pepper

¼ teaspoon celery salt

Dash salt

Dash ground red pepper (cayenne)

6 slices bacon, crisply cooked, crumbled

¾ cup shredded Cheddar cheese (3 oz)

1 egg yolk

1 tablespoon water

1 tablespoon sesame seed

TOPPINGS

1 cup chopped romaine lettuce

1 medium tomato, seeded, finely chopped

¼ cup chopped green onions (4 medium)

1 Heat oven to 400°F. Line cookie sheet with heavy-duty foil. Unroll pie crust; place crust flat between 2 sheets of waxed paper. With rolling pin, roll crust into 14 × 12-inch oval. Remove top waxed paper; carefully turn pie crust over onto cookie sheet. Remove waxed paper.

2 Spread 2 tablespoons of the mayonnaise evenly over crust to within 2 inches of edge. Sprinkle Monterey Jack cheese over mayonnaise.

3 In small bowl, mix chicken, remaining 2 tablespoons mayonnaise, the mustard, lemon juice, black pepper, celery salt, salt and ground red pepper. Spoon mixture over Monterey Jack cheese. Sprinkle with crumbled bacon. Sprinkle Cheddar cheese over top.

4 Fold 2-inch edge of crust up over filling, pleating crust as necessary and leaving 5 × 7-inch oval opening in center. Gently press down on edge to securely enclose filling.

5 In small bowl, beat egg yolk and water with fork. Generously brush yolk mixture over crust; sprinkle crust with sesame seed.

6 Bake 20 to 25 minutes or until crust is golden brown. Cool 10 minutes. With metal spatula, gently lift edge; slide onto serving plate. Sprinkle lettuce over filling; press down lightly. Top with tomato and onions. Cut into 6 wedges to serve.

High Altitude (3500–6500 ft): No change.

1 Serving: Calories 630; Total Fat 42g (Saturated Fat 16g; Trans Fat 0g); Cholesterol 120mg; Sodium 860mg; Total Carbohydrate 37g (Dietary Fiber 0g) **Exchanges:** 1 Starch, 1½ Other Carbohydrate, 3½ Medium-Fat Meat, 4½ Fat **Carbohydrate Choices:** 2½

savory crescent chicken squares

4 SANDWICHES

PREP TIME: *20 minutes*

START TO FINISH: *50 minutes*

DORIS CASTLE

River Forest, IL

Bake-Off® Contest 25, 1974

1 Heat oven to 350°F. In medium bowl, mix cream cheese and 1 table-spoon softened butter; beat until smooth. Stir in chicken, chives, salt, pepper, milk and pimientos; mix well.

2 If using crescent rolls: Unroll dough; separate into 4 rectangles. Firmly press perforations to seal. If using dough sheet: Unroll dough; cut into 4 rectangles.

3 Spoon ½ cup chicken mixture onto center of each rectangle. Pull 4 cor-ners of dough to center of chicken mixture; twist firmly. Pinch edges to seal. Place on ungreased cookie sheet. Brush tops of sandwiches with 1 tablespoon melted butter; sprinkle with crushed croutons.

4 Bake 25 to 30 minutes or until golden brown.

High Altitude (3500–6500 ft): Bake 27 to 32 minutes.

Photo on page 6.

1 package (3 oz) cream cheese, softened

1 tablespoon butter or margarine, softened

2 cups cubed cooked chicken

1 tablespoon chopped fresh chives or onion

¼ teaspoon salt

⅛ teaspoon pepper

2 tablespoons milk

1 tablespoon chopped pimientos, if desired

1 can (8 oz) Pillsbury refrigerated crescent dinner rolls or 1 can (8 oz) Pillsbury Crescent Recipe Creations refrigerated flaky dough sheet

1 tablespoon butter or margarine, melted

¾ cup seasoned croutons, crushed

1 Sandwich: Calories 500; Total Fat 32g (Saturated Fat 12g; Trans Fat 6g); Cholesterol 85mg; Sodium 870mg; Total Carbohydrate 28g (Dietary Fiber 1g) **Exchanges:** 1½ Starch, ½ Other Carbohydrate, 3 Medium-Fat Meat, 3 Fat **Carbohydrate Choices:** 2

taco-ranch-chicken sandwiches

JENNY FLAKE
Gilbert, AZ
Bake-Off® Contest 41, 2004

8 SERVINGS

PREP TIME: *45 minutes*
START TO FINISH: *1 hour 10 minutes*

1 tablespoon extra-virgin olive oil

2 medium boneless skinless chicken breasts, cut into small cubes (about 1½ cups)

¼ cup finely chopped red onion

2½ tablespoons taco seasoning mix (from 1-oz package)

1½ cups ranch dressing

1 cup finely shredded Cheddar cheese (4 oz)

1 medium plum (Roma) tomato, diced (½ cup)

1 tablespoon chopped fresh cilantro

1 clove garlic, finely chopped (½ teaspoon)

1 can (16.3 oz) Pillsbury Grands! Homestyle refrigerated buttermilk biscuits

1 tablespoon grated Parmesan cheese

2 cups shredded iceberg lettuce

1 Heat oven to 375°F. Lightly spray large cookie sheet with cooking spray. In 10-inch nonstick skillet, heat oil over medium heat until hot. Add chicken and onion; sprinkle with 1 rounded teaspoon of the taco seasoning mix, and mix thoroughly. Cook 5 to 7 minutes, stirring frequently, until chicken is no longer pink in center. Remove from heat.

2 In medium bowl, mix ranch dressing and 2 tablespoons of the taco seasoning mix until well blended. Place 1 cup dressing mixture in small serving bowl; set aside. To remaining salad dressing mixture in medium bowl, stir in Cheddar cheese, tomato, cilantro, garlic and chicken mixture.

3 Separate dough into 8 biscuits. Place 4 biscuits on cookie sheet; with fingers, press each into 5-inch round. Place rounded ½ cup chicken mixture on center of each biscuit. Press remaining 4 biscuits into 5-inch rounds; place over topped biscuits on cookie sheet, making sure top and bottom edges match up. Press edges firmly to seal.

4 Lift edges of filled biscuits off cookie sheet, and with scissors, snip edges ¼ inch deep and ½ inch apart all the way around to make a fringed look. In small bowl, mix Parmesan cheese and ⅛ teaspoon of the taco seasoning mix. Rub cheese mixture over tops of biscuits.

5 Bake 16 to 22 minutes or until deep golden brown. Cool on cookie sheet 3 to 5 minutes. Meanwhile, place serving bowl of dressing mixture in center of large platter; arrange shredded lettuce around bowl.

6 Remove sandwiches from cookie sheet Cut each sandwich in half. Arrange sandwich halves on lettuce around bowl of sauce.

High Altitude (3500–6500 ft): No change.

1 Serving (½ Sandwich and 2 Tablespoons Sauce): Calories 540; Total Fat 39g (Saturated Fat 10g; Trans Fat 3.5g); Cholesterol 50mg; Sodium 1230mg; Total Carbohydrate 31g (Dietary Fiber 1g) **Exchanges:** 1½ Starch, ½ Other Carbohydrate, 1½ Lean Meat, 6 Fat **Carbohydrate Choices:** 2

caesar chicken salad squares

LISA HUFF
Birmingham, AL
Bake-Off® Contest 41, 2004

4 SERVINGS
PREP TIME: *15 minutes*
START TO FINISH: *40 minutes*

FILLING

2 cups cubed (⅛ to ¼ inch) cooked chicken breast or 1 can (12.5 oz) chunk chicken breast in water, drained

½ cup shredded mozzarella cheese or Italian cheese blend (2 oz)

1 tablespoon grated Parmesan cheese

1 tablespoon bacon flavor bits

2 tablespoons regular or reduced-fat Caesar dressing

1 tablespoon regular or reduced-fat mayonnaise

1 clove garlic, finely chopped

1 teaspoon lemon juice

CRUST

1 can (8 oz) Pillsbury refrigerated regular or reduced fat crescent dinner rolls or 1 can (8 oz) Pillsbury Crescent Recipe Creations refrigerated flaky dough sheet

GARNISH, IF DESIRED

¼ cup Caesar dressing

1 cup shredded romaine lettuce

1 Heat oven to 375°F. In medium bowl, mix filling ingredients until well blended.

2 If using crescent rolls: Unroll dough; separate into 4 rectangles. Place on ungreased cookie sheet; press each into 6 × 4-inch rectangle. Firmly press perforations to seal. If using dough sheet: Unroll dough; cut into 4 rectangles. Place on ungreased cookie sheet; press each into 6 × 4-inch rectangle.

3 Spoon about ½ cup filling onto center of each rectangle. With knife, cut each corner of each rectangle from edge to within ½ inch of filling. Bring the 8 points of each rectangle up over filling; firmly pinch to seal, forming a square.

4 Bake 16 to 21 minutes or until deep golden brown. Remove from cookie sheet. Garnish each with 1 tablespoon Caesar dressing and ¼ cup shredded lettuce.

High Altitude (3500–6500 ft): No change.

1 Serving: Calories 440; Total Fat 26g (Saturated Fat 8g; Trans Fat 3g); Cholesterol 70mg; Sodium 740mg; Total Carbohydrate 23g (Dietary Fiber 0g) **Exchanges:** 1½ Starch, 3½ Medium-Fat Meat, 1½ Fat **Carbohydrate Choices:** 1½

beale street chicken braid

MANDY MYERS

Clarksville, AR

Bake-Off® Contest 41, 2004

4 SERVINGS

PREP TIME: *15 minutes*

START TO FINISH: *35 minutes*

1 medium Granny Smith apple, peeled, thinly sliced

1 small sweet onion, thinly sliced

1½ tablespoons packed brown sugar

1 can (13.8 oz) Pillsbury refrigerated classic pizza crust

4 slices (1 oz each) provolone cheese, each cut into quarters

1 cup refrigerated honey hickory barbecue sauce with shredded chicken (from 18-oz container)

4 oz marbled mild Cheddar and white Cheddar cheese blend, cut into 12 slices

1 egg white, beaten

1 Heat oven to 425°F. Spray large cookie sheet and 10-inch skillet with cooking spray. Add apple and onion to skillet; cook over medium heat, stirring occasionally, until apple is tender and onion is translucent. Stir in brown sugar. Cook and stir 2 minutes longer. Remove from heat.

2 Unroll dough; place on cookie sheet. Starting at center, press out dough into 15 × 10-inch rectangle. Place provolone cheese slices in 5-inch-wide strip down center of dough. Spoon barbecue sauce with shredded chicken over cheese. Layer apple-onion mixture over chicken. Arrange Cheddar cheese blend slices evenly over apple-onion mixture.

3 With scissors or sharp knife, make cuts 1 inch apart on long sides of dough rectangle to within ½ inch of filling. Alternately cross strips diagonally over filling; turn ends under, and press to seal. Brush beaten egg white over top.

4 Bake 11 to 15 minutes or until crust is deep golden brown. Let stand 5 minutes before serving. Remove from cookie sheet; cut into crosswise slices.

High Altitude (3500–6500 ft): No change.

1 Serving: Calories 600; Total Fat 22g (Saturated Fat 12g; Trans Fat 0g); Cholesterol 65mg; Sodium 1590mg; Total Carbohydrate 70g (Dietary Fiber 2g) **Exchanges:** 3 Starch, 1½ Other Carbohydrate, 3 Medium-Fat Meat, 1 Fat **Carbohydrate Choices:** 4½

Poblanos Florentine Casserole (page 115) ▶

www.pillsbury.com

tasty tuna biscuit casserole

MRS. MARY BARSON

Oklahoma City, OK

Bake-Off® Contest 23, 1972

4 SERVINGS

PREP TIME: *15 minutes*

START TO FINISH: *45 minutes*

1 can (9 to 12 oz) tuna, drained

1 cup shredded American or Cheddar cheese (4 oz)

1 can (10¾ oz) condensed cream of mushroom soup

1 cup frozen sweet peas or 1 can (8.5 oz) sweet peas, drained

½ cup green goddess dressing or other creamy dressing

½ cup milk

3 tablespoons chopped onion or 2 teaspoons instant minced onion

1 can (7.5 oz) Pillsbury refrigerated buttermilk or Country biscuits

2 tablespoons butter or margarine, melted

½ cup crushed potato chips

1 Heat oven to 375°F. In ungreased shallow 2-quart casserole or 9-inch square pan, arrange tuna and sprinkle with cheese. In 2-quart saucepan, heat soup, peas, dressing, milk and onion just to boiling. Reduce heat; simmer uncovered, stirring occasionally, while preparing biscuits.

2 Separate dough into 10 biscuits Cut each biscuit into fourths. Pour hot soup mixture over tuna and cheese; arrange biscuit pieces over soup mixture. Brush with melted butter; sprinkle with potato chips.

3 Bake 30 to 40 minutes or until golden brown

High Altitude (3500–6500 ft): Place casserole in oven on cookie sheet with sides in case of spillover. Bake 35 to 40 minutes.

1 Serving: Calories 630; Total Fat 38g (Saturated Fat 13g; Trans Fat 0.5g); Cholesterol 75mg; Sodium 2010mg; Total Carbohydrate 44g (Dietary Fiber 2g) **Exchanges:** 1½ Starch, 1 Other Carbohydrate, ½ Vegetable, 2 Lean Meat, 1 High-Fat Meat, 5 Fat **Carbohydrate Choices:** 3

scalloped tuna and potato casserole

8 SERVINGS

PREP TIME: *10 minutes*

START TO FINISH: *1 hour 5 minutes*

MRS. MARGARET CARLSON
Brule, WI
Bake-Off® Contest 25, 1974

1 Heat oven to 400°F. In ungreased 2½- or 3-quart casserole, mix all ingredients except 1½ tablespoons of the sauce mix from potato package and the tomatoes.

2 Bake, uncovered, 40 to 45 minutes or until potatoes are tender. Garnish with tomatoes. Sprinkle with reserved sauce mix. Bake 5 to 8 minutes longer or until lightly browned.

High Altitude (3500–6500 ft): No change.

1 box (4.9 oz) scalloped or au gratin potatoes

¼ cup chopped onion or 1 tablespoon dried minced onion

1 cup hot water

1 cup milk

¾ cup cottage cheese

2 tablespoons butter or margarine

2 tablespoons chopped pimientos, if desired

2 cups frozen sweet peas, partially thawed

1 can (5 to 6 oz) tuna, drained

1 can (10¾ oz) condensed cream of mushroom soup

2 tomatoes, sliced or quartered, if desired

1 Serving: Calories 160; Total Fat 8g (Saturated Fat 4g; Trans Fat 0g); Cholesterol 20mg; Sodium 490mg; Total Carbohydrate 12g (Dietary Fiber 1g) **Exchanges:** 1 Starch, 1 Lean Meat, ½ Fat **Carbohydrate Choices:** 1

cravin' crab enchiladas

SHARON CHITTOCK

Grass Valley, CA

Bake-Off® Contest 43, 2008

10 SERVINGS

PREP TIME: *40 minutes*

START TO FINISH: *1 hour 25 minutes*

ENCHILADAS

1 can (19 oz) mild enchilada sauce

1 cup whipping cream

2 tablespoons olive oil

¼ cup coarsely chopped onion

1 box (10 oz) frozen corn in a butter sauce, thawed

1 can (4.5 oz) chopped green chiles

½ cup lightly packed fresh cilantro, stems removed, coarsely chopped

¼ cup dry sherry or apple juice

1 can (1 lb) pasteurized crabmeat or 3 cans (6 oz each) lump crabmeat, drained

1 package (8.2 oz) flour tortillas for soft tacos & fajitas (10 tortillas)

4 cups shredded Cheddar-Monterey Jack or Colby–Monterey Jack cheese blend (1 lb)

½ cup chopped green onions (about 8 medium)

1 package (2 oz) slivered blanched almonds

GARNISHES

⅔ cup sour cream

Lime wedges

1 Heat oven to 350°F. Spray 13 × 9-inch (3-quart) glass baking dish with cooking spray.

2 In 2-quart saucepan, heat enchilada sauce and whipping cream to boiling over medium heat, stirring occasionally. Reduce heat; simmer uncovered 7 to 10 minutes, stirring occasionally, until sauce is reduced and slightly thickened.

3 Meanwhile, in 12-inch skillet, heat oil over medium-high heat until hot. Add onion; cook 2 to 3 minutes, stirring occasionally, until softened and translucent (do not brown). Stir in corn, chiles, ¼ cup of the cilantro, the sherry and crabmeat until well mixed. Remove from heat.

4 Spoon slightly less than ½ cup crabmeat mixture down center of each tortilla; top each with ¼ cup of the cheese. Roll up tortillas; place seam sides down in baking dish. Sprinkle remaining 1½ cups cheese over enchiladas. Pour sauce mixture over enchiladas.

5 Bake 30 to 35 minutes or until bubbly around edges. Sprinkle with remaining ¼ cup cilantro, the green onions and almonds. Serve with sour cream and lime wedges.

High Altitude (3500–6500 ft): No change.

1 Serving (1 Enchilada): Calories 530; Total Fat 35g (Saturated Fat 17g; Trans Fat 1.5g); Cholesterol 130mg; Sodium 990mg; Total Carbohydrate 26g (Dietary Fiber 2g) **Exchanges:** 1 Starch, ½ Other Carbohydrate, 3½ Medium-Fat Meat, 3½ Fat **Carbohydrate Choices:** 2

salmon fluff casserole

MRS. ANN VAN DOREN
Webster, NY
Bake-Off® Contest 21, 1970

8 SERVINGS
PREP TIME: *15 minutes*
START TO FINISH: *55 minutes*

CASSEROLE

1 can (14.75 oz) salmon, drained, flaked

8 saltine crackers, finely crushed (⅓ cup)

⅓ cup chopped onion or 1 tablespoon dried minced onion

1 teaspoon salt

⅛ teaspoon pepper

⅓ cup milk

1 egg

1 can (14.5 oz) diced tomatoes, drained

1 cup shredded Cheddar or American cheese (4 oz)

TOPPING

3 eggs

½ cup Pillsbury BEST all-purpose flour*

½ teaspoon salt

⅛ teaspoon pepper

¾ cup sour cream

*If using Pillsbury BEST self-rising flour, omit salt in topping.

1 Heat oven to 350°F. Grease or spray bottom and sides of 8-inch square (2-quart) glass baking dish. In large bowl, mix all casserole ingredients except tomatoes and cheese. Lightly press mixture in pan. Place diced tomatoes on top; sprinkle with cheese.

2 Separate eggs, placing whites in deep small bowl, yolks in large bowl. To yolks in large bowl, add flour, salt, pepper and sour cream; beat with electric mixer on medium speed until thick and creamy. In deep small bowl, beat egg whites with electric mixer on high speed until stiff but not dry. Using spatula or rubber scraper, fold whites gently, but thoroughly, into sour cream mixture. Pour mixture over cheese, spreading to cover.

3 Bake 30 to 35 minutes or until golden brown. Let stand 5 minutes before serving. Serve hot.

High Altitude (3500–6500 ft): No change.

1 Serving: Calories 250; Total Fat 14g (Saturated Fat 7g; Trans Fat 0g); Cholesterol 170mg; Sodium 840mg; Total Carbohydrate 12g (Dietary Fiber 0g) **Exchanges:** 1 Starch, 2½ Medium-Fat Meat **Carbohydrate Choices:** 1

crescent cod bake

8 SERVINGS

PREP TIME: *20 minutes*
START TO FINISH: *1 hour*

GAILE M. TRIPP (MRS. JERRY)
Mora, MN
Bake-Off® Contest 29, 1980

1   Heat oven to 350°F. In 4-quart saucepan over medium-high heat, heat water and lemon to boiling. Cut fish into 2 or 3 pieces to fit pan; add to boiling water. Return to boiling. Reduce heat; simmer covered 10 minutes, stirring occasionally. Drain well; flake fish with fork. In medium bowl, mix soup, milk and mushrooms; stir in flaked fish. Pour mixture into ungreased 10-inch glass pie plate or 9-inch square pan.

2   Separate dough into 8 triangles. Spoon rounded tablespoonful cheese on wide end of each triangle. Fold corners over cheese and roll 2 turns; seal ends. Arrange in circle over fish mixture with dough points joining in center.**

3   Bake 30 to 40 minutes or until golden brown. (Place pie plate on foil or cookie sheet during last 10 minutes of baking to guard against spillage.)

**To make ahead, prepare, cover and refrigerate up to 2 hours; bake as directed.

High Altitude (3500–6500 ft): No change.

4 cups water

½ lemon, cut into quarters

1¼ to 1½ lb frozen cod fillets

1 can (10.75 oz) condensed cream of shrimp soup

¼ cup evaporated milk or half-and-half

1 jar (4.5 oz) sliced mushrooms, drained, if desired

1 can (8 oz) Pillsbury refrigerated crescent dinner rolls

¾ cup shredded Cheddar cheese (3 oz)*

*3 oz of cheese cut into eight
2 × ¼-inch strips can be substituted.

1 Serving: Calories 250; Total Fat 13g (Saturated Fat 5g; Trans Fat 1.5g); Cholesterol 55mg; Sodium 630mg; Total Carbohydrate 14g (Dietary Fiber 0g) **Exchanges:** 1 Starch, 2½ Medium-Fat Meat **Carbohydrate Choices:** 1

seafood fantasy

MRS. VIRGINIA SANTOSUOSSO
West Rosbury, MA
Bake-Off® Contest 14, 1962

6 SERVINGS

PREP TIME: *20 minutes*
START TO FINISH: *55 minutes*

CASEROLE

1 box (9 oz) frozen spinach, thawed, squeezed to drain

¼ cup butter or margarine

1 jar (2.5 oz) sliced mushrooms, drained

2 tablespoons Pillsbury BEST all-purpose flour

½ teaspoon salt

⅛ teaspoon white or black pepper

2 cups milk

½ cup half-and-half

1 cup shredded Swiss cheese

2 cans (6 oz each) crabmeat, drained, cartilage removed*

¼ cup chopped slivered or sliced almonds, toasted**

PARSLEY BISCUITS

1 cup Pillsbury BEST all-purpose flour***

1½ teaspoons sugar

1½ teaspoons baking powder

½ teaspoon salt

¼ cup butter or margarine

2 tablespoons chopped fresh parsley or 2 teaspoons parsley flakes

⅓ cup half-and-half

1 egg

1 Heat oven to 425°F. In 8-inch square (2-quart) glass baking dish or 2-quart casserole, arrange spinach.

2 In 2-quart saucepan, melt butter over medium heat. Cook mushrooms in butter, stirring occasionally, until tender. Stir in 2 tablespoons flour, ½ teaspoon salt and the pepper. Gradually add 2 cups milk. Cook over medium heat, stirring constantly, until thickened.

3 Add ½ cup half-and-half and the cheese, stirring until cheese melts. Remove from heat. Stir in crabmeat and almonds; pour over spinach.

4 In medium bowl, mix 1 cup flour, the sugar, baking powder and ½ teaspoon salt. Cut in butter, using pastry blender (or pulling 2 table knives through mixture in opposite directions), until mixture looks like fine crumbs. Stir in parsley, ⅓ cup half-and-half and the egg, stirring just until flour is moistened. Drop by teaspoonfuls evenly over crabmeat mixture.

5 Bake 25 to 30 minutes or until golden brown.

*2 cans (6 oz each) tiny shrimp, drained, can be substituted for the crabmeat.

**To toast almonds, heat oven to 350°F. Spread almonds in ungreased shallow pan. Bake uncovered 6 to 10 minutes, stirring occasionally, until light brown. Or sprinkle in ungreased heavy skillet. Cook over medium heat 5 to 7 minutes, stirring frequently until nuts begin to brown, then stirring constantly until nuts are light brown.

***If using Pillsbury BEST self-rising flour, omit baking powder and salt in biscuits.

High Altitude (3500–6500 ft): No change.

1 Serving: Calories 480; Total Fat 30g (Saturated Fat 17g; Trans Fat 1g); Cholesterol 150mg; Sodium 920mg; Total Carbohydrate 28g (Dietary Fiber 2g) **Exchanges:** 2 Starch, 2½ Medium-Fat Meat, 3 Fat **Carbohydrate Choices:** 2

creole crescent shrimp bake

6 SERVINGS

PREP TIME: *15 minutes*

START TO FINISH: *55 minutes*

MRS. CHARLA RUDOLPH
Santa Ana, CA
Bake-Off® Contest 27, 1976

1 Heat oven to 350°F. Separate dough into 2 rectangles. Place in ungreased 13 × 9-inch pan; press dough over bottom and ½ inch up sides to form crust. Firmly press perforations to seal.

2 In medium bowl, beat eggs and soup with whisk or fork; blend in remaining ingredients. Spoon mixture over crust.

3 Bake 32 to 38 minutes until edges are brown and filling is set.

High Altitude (3500–6500 ft): No change.

1 can (8 oz) Pillsbury refrigerated crescent dinner rolls

3 eggs

1 can (10¾ oz) condensed tomato soup

¾ cup chopped onions or 3 tablespoons dried minced onion

½ cup chopped green bell pepper

1 package (12 oz) frozen cooked deveined peeled shrimp, thawed, or 2 cans (6 oz each) tiny shrimp, drained

2 cups shredded Swiss or Monterey Jack cheese (8 oz)

½ teaspoon salt

¼ teaspoon garlic powder

½ teaspoon celery seed, if desired

1 Serving: Calories 400; Total Fat 22g (Saturated Fat 10g; Trans Fat 2.5g); Cholesterol 200mg; Sodium 970mg; Total Carbohydrate 27g (Dietary Fiber 1g) **Exchanges:** 2 Starch, 2½ Medium-Fat Meat, 1½ Fat **Carbohydrate Choices:** 2

shrimp enchiladas
with sweet corn sauce

BARBARA HAHN
Park Hills, MO
Bake-Off® Contest 43, 2008

4 SERVINGS
PREP TIME: *35 minutes*
START TO FINISH: *1 hour 5 minutes*

SAUCE

1 box (10 oz) frozen corn in a butter sauce

1 can (4.5 oz) chopped green chiles

1 tablespoon sugar

¼ cup lightly packed fresh cilantro sprigs

¾ cup milk

ENCHILADAS

1 tablespoon light olive oil

1 teaspoon lime juice

12 oz uncooked medium shrimp (about 24), thawed if frozen, peeled and deveined

½ teaspoon ground cumin

1 cup refrigerated cooked shredded hash brown potatoes (from 20-oz bag)

¼ cup diced red bell pepper

1 jalapeño chile, seeded, diced

2 cups shredded Mexican cheese blend (8 oz)

8 flour tortillas for soft tacos & fajitas (from 8.2-oz package)

Finely chopped red cabbage, if desired

Finely chopped green onions, if desired

1 Heat oven to 350°F. Spray 13 × 9-inch (3-quart) glass baking dish with cooking spray.

2 Cook corn in microwave as directed on package.

3 In blender or food processor, place 1 cup of the corn and butter sauce, 3 tablespoons of the green chiles, the sugar, cilantro and milk. Cover; blend on medium speed until creamy. Pour into medium bowl; stir in remaining corn and butter sauce until well mixed. Set aside.

4 In 10-inch nonstick skillet, heat oil and lime juice over medium-high heat. Add shrimp; sprinkle cumin over shrimp. Cook 2 to 3 minutes, turning once, until shrimp are pink. Remove shrimp from skillet to cutting board; chop. Set aside.

5 In same skillet, cook potatoes over medium heat 4 to 5 minutes, turning occasionally, until thoroughly heated. Remove from heat. Stir in shrimp, remaining green chiles, the bell pepper, jalapeño chile and cheese until mixed.

6 Heat tortillas in microwave as directed on package.

7 Pour half of the corn sauce in bottom of baking dish. Spoon about ½ cup shrimp mixture down center of each tortilla. Roll up each tortilla; place seam side down on corn sauce in baking dish. Pour remaining corn sauce evenly over enchiladas.

8 Bake 25 to 30 minutes or until thoroughly heated. To serve, place 2 enchiladas on each of 4 serving plates. Garnish with cabbage and onions.

High Altitude (3500–6500 ft): Heat oven to 375°F.

1 Serving (2 Enchiladas): Calories 630; Total Fat 29g (Saturated Fat 14g; Trans Fat 2g); Cholesterol 175mg; Sodium 1310mg; Total Carbohydrate 59g (Dietary Fiber 4g) **Exchanges:** 3 Starch, 1 Other Carbohydrate, 3½ Lean Meat, 3 Fat **Carbohydrate Choices:** 4

louisiana shrimp bake

MRS. LAWRENCE C. DAVIS
Omaha, NE
Bake-Off® Contest 13, 1961

6 SERVINGS
PREP TIME: *20 minutes*
START TO FINISH: *40 minutes*

SHRIMP MIXTURE

¼ cup butter or margarine

¼ cup Pillsbury BEST all-purpose flour*

1 can (14.5 oz) diced tomatoes, undrained

¼ cup water

4 hard-cooked eggs, sliced

1 can (6 oz) tiny shrimp, drained, or 1 cup chopped cooked shrimp

½ cup chopped celery

½ cup chopped onion

¼ cup chopped green bell pepper

½ teaspoon salt*

½ teaspoon seasoned salt

½ teaspoon paprika

⅛ teaspoon pepper

1¼ cups shredded Cheddar cheese

CHEESE PASTRY

1 cup Pillsbury BEST all-purpose flour*

2 teaspoons baking powder

¼ teaspoon celery salt or salt*

1 tablespoon chopped fresh or ½ teaspoon parsley flakes

¼ to ½ teaspoon celery seed, if desired

3 tablespoons butter or margarine

⅓ cup half-and-half

*If using Pillsbury BEST self-rising flour in shrimp mixture, omit the ½ teaspoon salt. If using self-rising flour in cheese pastry, omit celery salt or salt.

1 Heat oven to 425°F. In 2-quart saucepan, melt ¼ cup butter over medium heat. Add ¼ cup flour; mix well. Gradually stir in diced tomatoes and water. Cook over medium heat, stirring constantly, until slightly thickened.

2 Stir in hard-cooked eggs, shrimp, celery, onion, bell pepper, ½ teaspoon salt, seasoned salt, paprika, pepper and 1 cup of the cheese. Cook and stir until hot. Pour into ungreased 1½- or 2-quart casserole.

3 In medium bowl, mix 1 cup flour, the baking powder and ¼ teaspoon celery salt. Stir in parsley, celery seed and remaining cheese. Cut in butter, using pastry blender (or pulling 2 table knives through mixture in opposite directions), until mixture looks like fine crumbs. Stir in half-and-half until dough leaves side of bowl. Place dough on lightly floured surface. Roll or pat ½ inch thick. Using sharp knife, score dough into 6 wedges. Place on top of casserole.

4 Bake 15 to 20 minutes or until pastry is golden brown.

High Altitude (3500–6500 ft): Increase water to ½ cup. Bake 25 to 30 minutes.

1 Serving: Calories 420; Total Fat 27g (Saturated Fat 16g; Trans Fat 1g); Cholesterol 280mg; Sodium 940mg; Total Carbohydrate 25g (Dietary Fiber 2g) **Exchanges:** 1½ Starch, 2 Medium-Fat Meat, 3 Fat **Carbohydrate Choices:** 1½

poblanos florentine casserole

9 SERVINGS

PREP TIME: *45 minutes*

START TO FINISH: *2 hours 5 minutes*

GLORIA FELTS
Indianapolis, IN
Bake-Off® Contest 43, 2008

1 Set oven control to broil. On cookie sheet, broil chiles with tops 2 inches from heat about 10 minutes, turning frequently with tongs, until all sides are blackened and blistered. Place chiles in paper bag; seal bag. Let chiles steam 15 minutes.

2 Heat oven to 350°F. Lightly spray 8-inch square (2-quart) glass baking dish with cooking spray.

3 In medium bowl, mix Chihuahua cheese and Mexican cheese blend. Reserve ¾ cup for topping. In another medium bowl, mix ricotta cheese, garlic, cumin and spinach. Stir in remaining shredded cheeses. Set aside.

4 Wearing food-safe plastic gloves, peel blackened skin from chiles. Cut open chiles; remove stems, seeds and membranes. Cut each chile in half lengthwise into 2 pieces; pat dry.

5 Separate dough into 10 biscuits. Separate each biscuit into 2 layers; flatten slightly.

6 Pour half of the enchilada sauce over bottom of baking dish. Place 10 biscuit layers on sauce, cutting biscuits if necessary to fit into dish. Top with 5 chile halves; spread spinach mixture over chiles. Top with remaining 5 chile halves and remaining 10 biscuit layers. Pour remaining enchilada sauce over biscuits.

7 Spray sheet of foil large enough to cover baking dish with cooking spray. Cover baking dish with foil, sprayed side down. Bake 55 to 60 minutes or until thoroughly heated and bubbly around edges.

8 Sprinkle with reserved ¾ cup shredded cheeses. Bake uncovered 5 to 8 minutes longer or until cheese is melted. Cool 10 minutes before cutting. Top each serving with tomatoes, guacamole and sour cream.

High Altitude (3500–6500 ft): No change.

Photo on page 103.

1 Serving: Calories 290; Total Fat 16g (Saturated Fat 8g; Trans Fat 2g); Cholesterol 30mg; Sodium 790mg; Total Carbohydrate 23g (Dietary Fiber 1g) **Exchanges:** 1 Starch, ½ Other Carbohydrate, 1 High-Fat Meat, 1½ Fat **Carbohydrate Choices:** 1½

---

5 fresh poblano chiles (4½ × 3 inch)

1½ cups shredded Chihuahua or Monterey Jack cheese (6 oz)

1 cup shredded Mexican cheese blend (4 oz)

⅓ cup ricotta cheese

2 cloves garlic, finely chopped

½ teaspoon ground cumin

1 box (9 oz) frozen spinach, thawed, squeezed to drain

1 can (12 oz) Pillsbury Grands! Jr. Golden Layers refrigerated biscuits

1 can (10 oz) mild enchilada sauce

2 plum (Roma) tomatoes, chopped, if desired

½ cup fresh guacamole, if desired

½ cup sour cream, if desired

pineapple–black bean enchiladas

MARY IOVINELLI BUESCHER
Bloomington, MN
Bake-Off® Contest 42, 2006

8 SERVINGS

PREP TIME: *30 minutes*
START TO FINISH: *1 hour 10 minutes*

2 teaspoons vegetable oil

1 large yellow onion, chopped (about 1 cup)

1 medium red bell pepper, chopped (about 1 cup)

1 can (20 oz) pineapple tidbits in juice, drained, ⅓ cup juice reserved

1 can (15 oz) black beans, drained, rinsed

1 can (4.5 oz) chopped green chiles

1 teaspoon salt

½ cup chopped fresh cilantro

3 cups shredded reduced-fat Cheddar cheese (12 oz)

1 can (10 oz) mild enchilada sauce

8 whole wheat flour tortillas (8 or 9 inch)

½ cup reduced-fat sour cream

8 teaspoons chopped fresh cilantro

1   Heat oven to 350°F. Spray 13 × 9-inch (3-quart) glass baking dish with cooking spray. In 12-inch nonstick skillet, heat oil over medium heat. Add onion and bell pepper; cook 4 to 5 minutes or until softened. Stir in pineapple, beans, green chiles and salt. Cook and stir until thoroughly heated. Remove from heat. Stir in ½ cup cilantro and 2 cups of the cheese.

2   Spoon and spread 1 tablespoon enchilada sauce onto each tortilla. Spoon about ¾ cup vegetable mixture over sauce on each. Roll up tortillas; place seam side down in baking dish.

3   In small bowl, mix reserved ⅓ cup pineapple juice and remaining enchilada sauce. Pour over entire surface of enchiladas in dish. Sprinkle with remaining 1 cup cheese. Spray sheet of foil large enough to cover baking dish with cooking spray; cover baking dish tightly with foil, sprayed side down.

4   Bake 35 to 40 minutes or until cheese is melted and sauce is bubbly, removing foil during last 5 to 10 minutes of baking, Top each baked enchilada with 1 tablespoon sour cream and 1 teaspoon cilantro.

High Altitude (3500–6500 ft): Bake 40 to 45 minutes, removing foil during last 5 to 10 minutes of baking.

1 Serving (1 Enchilada): Calories 330; Total Fat 7g (Saturated Fat 3g; Trans Fat 0g); Cholesterol 15mg; Sodium 1110mg; Total Carbohydrate 48g (Dietary Fiber 7g) **Exchanges:** 2 Starch, 1 Other Carbohydrate, 2 Lean Meat **Carbohydrate Choices:** 3

fiesta taco bake

PHOEBE JACKSON
Harleysville, PA
Bake-Off® Contest 37, 1996

5 SERVINGS
PREP TIME: *15 minutes*
START TO FINISH: *45 minutes*

CASSEROLE

1 jar (24 oz) chunky-style salsa

1 box (4.6 oz) taco shells (12 shells)

1 cup shredded Monterey Jack cheese (4 oz)

1 cup shredded Cheddar cheese (4 oz)

¼ cup chopped onion

1 can (11 oz) white shoepeg corn, drained

1 can (4.5 oz) chopped green chiles

1 can (15 oz) black beans, drained

2 teaspoons ground cumin

1 tablespoon steak sauce

½ cup sour cream

GARNISH, AS DESIRED

Fresh cilantro sprigs

Chopped fresh tomatoes

Sliced ripe olives

Chopped jalapeño chiles

Guacamole

Additional sour cream

1 Heat oven to 350°F. Spray 3-quart casserole with cooking spray. Spread 1 cup of the salsa in casserole. Break each taco shell into 4 to 6 pieces. Arrange half of the broken shells over salsa. Spread 1 cup of the remaining salsa over shells. Sprinkle with ½ cup each of the Monterey Jack and Cheddar cheeses. Top with onion, corn and green chiles.

2 In small bowl, stir together beans, cumin and steak sauce; spoon evenly over mixture in casserole. Top with remaining broken shells, Monterey Jack and Cheddar cheeses and salsa.

3 Cover; bake 20 minutes. Uncover; bake about 10 minutes longer or until bubbly and cheese is melted. Top with ½ cup sour cream; garnish with remaining ingredients.

High Altitude (3500–6500 ft): Heat oven to 375°F. Bake 25 minutes covered; uncover and bake about 5 minutes longer.

1 Serving: Calories 580; Total Fat 27g (Saturated Fat 13g; Trans Fat 2g); Cholesterol 60mg; Sodium 1810mg; Total Carbohydrate 62g (Dietary Fiber 14g) **Exchanges:** 3 Starch, 1 Other Carbohydrate, 2 Medium-Fat Meat, 3 Fat **Carbohydrate Choices:** 4

crab-in-a-custard

8 SERVINGS

PREP TIME: *20 minutes*

START TO FINISH: *1 hour 10 minutes*

MRS. RUTH E. CONWAY

Mariposa, CA

Bake-Off® Contest 17, 1966

1 Heat oven to 350°F. Grease or spray 9-inch square pan. In large bowl, beat flour, 1 teaspoon of the salt, the baking powder, sugar, 2 tablespoons of the butter, 1 egg and the milk with electric mixer on low speed about 1½ minutes or until smooth. Spread in pan. Spread crabmeat and bell pepper evenly over dough; sprinkle with cheese.

2 In large bowl, beat reserved crabmeat liquid, half-and-half, Worcestershire sauce, remaining ½ teaspoon salt and remaining 3 eggs with electric mixer on low speed until smooth and well blended.

3 Pour gently over crabmeat mixture. Spread crackers with remaining 1 tablespoon butter. Place on top of sauce, butter side up so pepper blend sticks; press each cracker into sauce just to moisten tops. Sprinkle with seasoned pepper blend.

4 Bake 40 to 45 minutes or until sauce is set and crackers are golden brown. Let stand 5 minutes before serving.

High Altitude (over 3500 ft): Not recommended.

1 cup Pillsbury BEST all-purpose or self-rising flour*

1½ teaspoons salt

1 teaspoon baking powder

1 teaspoon sugar

3 tablespoons butter or margarine, softened

4 eggs

½ cup milk

2 cans (6 oz each) crabmeat, drained and liquid reserved, cartilage removed

⅓ cup finely chopped green bell pepper

½ cup shredded Cheddar cheese (2 oz)

2 cups half-and-half

2 teaspoons Worcestershire sauce

16 saltine crackers

½ teaspoon seasoned pepper blend

*If using Pillsbury BEST® self-rising flour, omit the 1 teaspoon salt and the baking powder in step 1.

1 Serving: Calories 320; Total Fat 18g (Saturated Fat 10g; Trans Fat 0.5g); Cholesterol 185mg; Sodium 730mg; Total Carbohydrate 21g (Dietary Fiber 0g) **Exchanges:** 1½ Starch, 2 Lean Meat, 2 Fat **Carbohydrate Choices:** 1½

spinach and mushroom enchiladas with creamy red sauce

ROBIN HILL
Arlington, TX
Bake-Off® Contest 43, 2008

5 SERVINGS

PREP TIME: *45 minutes*

START TO FINISH: *1 hour 25 minutes*

1 can (10 oz) mild enchilada sauce

1 cup crema Mexicana table cream or sour cream

1 tablespoon olive oil

1 medium onion, chopped (½ cup)

3 cloves garlic, finely chopped

1 package (8 oz) sliced fresh baby portabella mushrooms

1 box (9 oz) frozen spinach, thawed, squeezed to drain

⅓ cup chopped drained roasted red bell peppers (from 7.25-oz jar)

2 tablespoons taco seasoning mix (from 1-oz package)

¼ cup lightly packed fresh cilantro sprigs

½ teaspoon ground cumin

1¼ cups shredded pepper Jack or salsa Jack cheese (5 oz)

2 cups shredded quesadilla or mozzarella cheese (8 oz)

1 package (8.2 oz) flour tortillas for soft tacos & fajitas (10 tortillas)

½ cup crumbled cotija cheese or fresh mozzarella cheese

1 Heat oven to 350°F. Spray 13 × 9-inch (3-quart) glass baking dish with cooking spray.

2 In 1-quart saucepan, heat enchilada sauce and ½ cup of the crema Mexicana over medium heat 2 to 3 minutes, stirring occasionally, until warm. Spread ¼ cup of the sauce mixture on bottom of baking dish. Set aside remaining sauce.

3 Meanwhile, in 12-inch nonstick skillet, heat oil over medium-high heat. Add onion and garlic; cook 2 to 3 minutes, stirring occasionally, until onion is tender. Stir in mushrooms; cook 7 to 8 minutes, stirring occasionally, until mushrooms are tender.

4 Transfer vegetable mixture to food processor bowl with metal blade. Add spinach, roasted peppers, taco seasoning mix, 2 tablespoons of the cilantro, the cumin and remaining ½ cup crema Mexicana. Cover; process with on-and-off pulses 6 to 8 times or until mushrooms are coarsely chopped. Pour mixture into large bowl; stir in pepper Jack cheese and 1¼ cups of the quesadilla cheese.

5 Spoon ⅓ cup vegetable filling down center of each tortilla. Roll up tortillas; place seam sides down on sauce in baking dish. Pour remaining sauce evenly over tortillas; sprinkle with remaining ¾ cup quesadilla cheese and the cotija cheese. Spray sheet of foil large enough to cover baking dish with cooking spray; cover baking dish tightly with foil, sprayed side down.

6 Bake 35 to 40 minutes or until thoroughly heated. Chop remaining 2 tablespoons cilantro; sprinkle over enchiladas before serving.

High Altitude (3500–6500 ft): Heat oven to 375°F.

1 Serving (2 Enchiladas): Calories 660; Total Fat 43g (Saturated Fat 23g; Trans Fat 2g); Cholesterol 110mg; Sodium 1660mg; Total Carbohydrate 41g (Dietary Fiber 3g) **Exchanges:** 2 Starch, ½ Other Carbohydrate, 1 Vegetable, 3 High-Fat Meat, 3 Fat **Carbohydrate Choices:** 3

tofu black bean enchiladas

PREP TIME: *20 minutes*
START TO FINISH: *50 minutes*

KATHY DORR
Fairport, NY
Bake-Off® Contest 40, 2002

1   Heat oven to 350°F. Spray 13 × 9-inch (3-quart) glass baking dish with cooking spray. In medium bowl, mix beans, corn, salsa, tofu, salt and red pepper sauce.

2   Spoon ⅓ cup tofu mixture down center of each warm tortilla; roll up. Place seam side down in baking dish. Pour enchilada sauce over enchiladas. Sprinkle cheese over top.

3   Bake 20 to 30 minutes or until enchiladas are hot and cheese is melted. Garnish with sour cream.

High Altitude (3500–6500 ft): No change.

1 can (15 oz) black beans, drained

1 can (11 oz) whole kernel corn with red and green peppers, drained

1 cup chunky-style salsa

5⅓ oz firm tofu, drained, cut into ¼-inch cubes (¾ cup)

½ teaspoon salt

⅛ teaspoon red pepper sauce

12 corn tortillas (6 inch), heated

1 can (10 oz) red enchilada sauce

2 cups shredded reduced-fat Cheddar cheese (8 oz)

1 cup reduced-fat sour cream, if desired

1 Serving (2 Enchiladas): Calories 360; Total Fat 6g (Saturated Fat 2.5g; Trans Fat 0g); Cholesterol 10mg; Sodium 1450mg; Total Carbohydrate 53g (Dietary Fiber 12g) **Exchanges:** 2½ Starch, 1 Other Carbohydrate, 2 Lean Meat **Carbohydrate Choices:** 3 ½

Seafood & Meatless Mainstays

broccoli-cauliflower tetrazzini

BARBARA VAN ITALLIE
Poughkeepsie, NY
Bake-Off® Contest 33, 1988

8 SERVINGS

PREP TIME: *30 minutes*
START TO FINISH: *50 minutes*

8 oz uncooked spaghetti, broken into thirds

1 bag (16 oz) frozen broccoli florets, cauliflower and carrots or 4 cups frozen cut broccoli

2 tablespoons butter or margarine

3 tablespoons Pillsbury BEST all-purpose flour

2 cups fat-free (skim) milk

½ cup grated Parmesan cheese

Dash pepper

1 jar (4.5 oz) sliced mushrooms, drained

2 tablespoons grated Parmesan cheese

1 Heat oven to 400°F. Grease or spray 13 x 9-inch (3-quart) glass baking dish.

2 Cook spaghetti as directed on package. Drain; rinse with hot water. Cover to keep warm; set aside. Cook vegetables until crisp-tender as directed on bag; drain.

3 In 2-quart saucepan, melt butter over medium heat. Stir in flour until smooth. Gradually add milk, cooking and stirring until well blended. Cook 6 to 10 minutes or until mixture boils and thickens, stirring constantly. Stir in ½ cup Parmesan cheese and the pepper.

4 Spoon cooked spaghetti into baking dish. Top with cooked vegetables and sliced mushrooms. Pour milk mixture over mushrooms. Sprinkle with 2 tablespoons Parmesan cheese.

5 Bake 15 to 20 minutes or until mixture bubbles around edges and is hot.

High Altitude (3500–6500 ft): Bake 20 to 30 minutes.

1 Serving: Calories 240; Total Fat 6g (Saturated Fat 3.5g; Trans Fat 0g); Cholesterol 15mg; Sodium 350mg; Total Carbohydrate 34g (Dietary Fiber 3g) **Exchanges:** 2 Starch, 1 Vegetable, ½ Lean Meat, ½ Fat **Carbohydrate Choices:** 2

deviled crab and cheese rolls

MICHAEL W. WEAVER

San Francisco, CA

Bake-Off® Contest 42, 2006

6 SANDWICHES

PREP TIME: *10 minutes*

START TO FINISH: *50 minutes*

½ cup whipped cream cheese spread (from 8-oz container)

1 tablespoon fresh lemon juice

1 to 2 teaspoons red pepper sauce

¼ cup finely shredded mild Cheddar cheese (1 oz)

2 tablespoons finely chopped green onions (2 medium)

1 teaspoon paprika

½ cup garlic-herb dry bread crumbs

3 cans (6 oz each) white crabmeat, well drained

1 can (11 oz) Pillsbury refrigerated original breadsticks

1 egg, slightly beaten

1 Heat oven to 350°F. Spray cookie sheet with cooking spray or line with a silicone baking mat. In medium bowl, mix cream cheese spread, lemon juice and pepper sauce until smooth. Stir in Cheddar cheese, onions and paprika. Reserve 2 tablespoons bread crumbs for topping. Stir remaining bread crumbs into cream cheese mixture. Gently stir in crabmeat. Shape crabmeat mixture into 6 balls, using about ⅓ cup mixture for each; flatten slightly.

2 Separate dough into 6 (2-breadstick) portions. Seal seam halfway up length of each portion; place 1 ball on sealed side of each. Holding dough and ball in one hand, stretch dough strips over balls, crisscrossing and tucking ends under opposite side; place on cookie sheet.

3 Lightly brush tops and sides of dough with beaten egg; sprinkle with reserved 2 tablespoons bread crumbs.

4 Bake 20 to 30 minutes or until golden brown. Cool 10 minutes. Serve warm.

High Altitude (3500–6500 ft): No change.

1 Sandwich: Calories 330; Total Fat 11g (Saturated Fat 5g; Trans Fat 0.5g); Cholesterol 120mg; Sodium 890mg; Total Carbohydrate 33g (Dietary Fiber 0g) **Exchanges:** 2 Starch, 2½ Lean Meat, ½ Fat **Carbohydrate Choices:** 2

gnocchi alfredo casserole

KELLY LYNNE BAXTER

Olympia, WA

Bake-Off® Contest 40, 2002

6 SERVINGS

PREP TIME: *15 minutes*

START TO FINISH: *50 minutes*

1 package (16 oz) potato gnocchi*

¼ cup butter or margarine

1 clove garlic, finely chopped

1 cup whipping cream

1½ cups shredded fresh Romano cheese (6 oz)

¼ lb cooked ham, coarsely chopped (¾ cup)

1 bag (10 oz) frozen cut broccoli in a cheese flavored sauce, thawed

2 jars (4.5 oz each) sliced mushrooms, drained

½ cup Parmesan bread crumbs

*Potato gnocchi, depending upon the brand, may be a refrigerated, frozen or shelf-stable product.

1 Heat oven to 400°F. Cook gnocchi as directed on package, omitting salt.

2 Meanwhile, in 10-inch nonstick skillet, melt butter over medium heat. Add garlic; cook and stir 3 minutes. Add cream; mix well. Gradually add 1 cup of the cheese, stirring after each addition until melted.

3 Add ham, broccoli and sauce, mushrooms and cooked gnocchi; mix well. Spoon into ungreased 1½-quart casserole. In small bowl, stir bread crumbs and remaining ½ cup cheese. Sprinkle over casserole.

4 Bake about 30 minutes or until golden brown. Cool 5 minutes before serving.

High Altitude (3500–6500 ft): No change.

1 Serving: Calories 540; Total Fat 41g (Saturated Fat 22g; Trans Fat 2.5g); Cholesterol 155mg; Sodium 1340mg; Total Carbohydrate 19g (Dietary Fiber 2g) **Exchanges:** 1 Starch, ½ Vegetable, 2½ Lean Meat, 6½ Fat **Carbohydrate Choices:** 1

Breakfast Quiches to Go (page 139) ▶

www.pillsbury.com

dinner pies & quiches

big tastin' sloppy joe pie

MRS. BRIAN L. SULLIVAN
Seattle, WA
Bake-Off® Contest 27, 1976

4 SERVINGS
PREP TIME: *20 minutes*
START TO FINISH: *50 minutes*

CASSEROLE
- 1 lb lean (at least 80%) ground beef
- ½ cup chopped onion or 2 tablespoons dried minced onion
- 1 can (8 oz) tomato sauce
- 1 can (7 oz) whole kernel corn, drained
- ¼ cup water or liquid from corn
- 1 package (1.31 oz) sloppy joe or chili seasoning mix

CRUST
- 1 can (10.2 oz) Pillsbury Grands! refrigerated biscuits (5 biscuits)
- 2 tablespoons milk
- ⅓ cup cornmeal
- 1 cup shredded Cheddar cheese (4 oz)

1 Heat oven to 375°F. In 10-inch skillet, cook beef and onion over medium heat 8 to 10 minutes, stirring occasionally, until beef is thoroughly cooked; drain. Stir in tomato sauce, corn, water and seasoning mix. Heat until hot and bubbly. Reduce heat; simmer uncovered while preparing crust.

2 Separate dough into 10 biscuits; flatten slightly. Dip each in milk; then in cornmeal. Arrange 7 biscuits around sides and 3 on bottom of ungreased 9- or 10-inch glass pie plate; press biscuits to form crust. (Biscuits will form petal-like shape around rim of pan.) Sprinkle crust with ½ cup of the cheese. Spoon hot beef mixture over cheese; sprinkle with remaining ½ cup cheese.

3 Bake 20 to 25 minutes or until crust is deep golden brown. Cool 5 minutes before serving.

High Altitude (3500–6500 ft): No change.

1 Serving: Calories 680; Total Fat 34g (Saturated Fat 13g; Trans Fat 5g); Cholesterol 100mg; Sodium 1940mg; Total Carbohydrate 57g (Dietary Fiber 2g) **Exchanges:** 4 Starch, 3 Medium-Fat Meat, 3 Fat **Carbohydrate Choices:** 4

layered italian beef pie

8 SERVINGS

PREP TIME: *30 minutes*
START TO FINISH: *1 hour 15 minutes*

RUTH BOUDREAUX
Broussard, LA
Bake-Off® Contest 32, 1986

1   Heat oven to 450°F. Make pie crust as directed on box for One-Crust Baked Shell, using 9-inch glass pie plate. Bake 9 to 11 minutes or until light golden brown. Reduce oven temperature to 350°F.

2   Meanwhile, in 10-inch skillet, cook beef over medium-high heat 5 to 7 minutes, stirring frequently, until thoroughly cooked; drain well. Add pasta sauce; mix well. Heat to boiling. Reduce heat; simmer uncovered about 10 minutes or until hot, stirring occasionally.

3   In medium bowl, beat eggs with whisk or fork until well blended. Add Parmesan cheese and spinach; mix well. Spoon half of beef mixture into baked shell. Sprinkle with 1 cup of the mozzarella cheese and ¼ cup of the olives. Spoon spinach mixture evenly over cheese. Top with remaining beef mixture.

4   Bake at 350°F 25 to 35 minutes or until filling is hot. If necessary, cover edge of crust with strips of foil after 15 to 20 minutes of baking to prevent excessive browning. Sprinkle pie with remaining 1 cup mozzarella cheese and ¼ cup olives. Bake 4 to 5 minutes longer or until cheese is melted. Let stand 5 minutes before serving.

High Altitude (3500–6500 ft): After topping pie with cheese and olives in step 4, bake 5 to 7 minutes longer.

1 Pillsbury refrigerated pie crust (from 15-oz box), softened as directed on box

1 lb lean (at least 80%) ground beef

1 cup tomato pasta sauce with mushrooms and onions, or other variety

2 eggs

¼ cup grated Parmesan cheese

1 box (9 oz) frozen spinach, thawed, squeezed to drain

2 cups shredded mozzarella cheese (8 oz)

½ cup sliced ripe olives

1 Serving: Calories 380; Total Fat 23g (Saturated Fat 10g; Trans Fat 0.5g); Cholesterol 110mg; Sodium 600mg; Total Carbohydrate 22g (Dietary Fiber 1g) **Exchanges:** 1 Starch, ½ Other Carbohydrate, 2½ Medium-Fat Meat, 2 Fat **Carbohydrate Choices:** 1½

southwestern chicken pie

HARRIET MATHIS
Orlando, FL
Bake-Off® Contest 39, 2000

6 SERVINGS

PREP TIME: *15 minutes*
START TO FINISH: *1 hour 10 minutes*

1 box (15 oz) Pillsbury refrigerated pie crusts, softened as directed on box

1 package (9 oz) frozen cooked southwestern-seasoned chicken breast strips, thawed, cut into bite-size pieces

½ cup uncooked instant white rice

1 can (15 oz) black beans, drained, rinsed

1 can (11 oz) whole kernel corn with red and green peppers, drained

1 can (2.25 oz) sliced ripe olives, drained

1 teaspoon garlic powder

1 teaspoon ground cumin

½ teaspoon salt

½ teaspoon pepper

1 cup sour cream

1 cup chunky-style salsa

2 cups shredded Colby–Monterey Jack cheese blend (8 oz)

1 egg, beaten

1 to 2 teaspoons chopped fresh parsley

1 Heat oven to 400°F. Prepare pie crusts as directed on box for Two-Crust Pie, using 9-inch glass pie plate.

2 In large bowl, mix remaining ingredients except egg and parsley. Pour into crust-lined pie plate. Top with second crust; seal edge and flute; cut slits in several places. Brush top with beaten egg; sprinkle with parsley.

3 Bake 38 to 48 minutes or until golden brown. Cover edge of crust with strips of foil after 15 to 20 minutes of baking to prevent excessive browning. Let stand 5 minutes before serving.

High Altitude (3500–6500 ft): Bake 50 to 55 minutes.

1 Serving: Calories 730; Total Fat 37g (Saturated Fat 16g; Trans Fat 0g); Cholesterol 115mg; Sodium 1650mg; Total Carbohydrate 73g (Dietary Fiber 9g) **Exchanges:** 3 Starch, 2 Other Carbohydrate, 2½ Lean Meat, 5½ Fat **Carbohydrate Choices:** 5

biscuit beef 'n corn combo

MRS. BRENDA PILLSBURY
Bath, ME
Bake-Off® Contest 23, 1972

4 SERVINGS
PREP TIME: *15 minutes*
START TO FINISH: *45 minutes*

1 lb lean (at least 80%) ground beef

½ cup chopped onion or 2 tablespoons instant minced onion

½ cup chopped green bell pepper

1 can (15.25 oz) whole kernel corn, drained

1 can (10¾ oz) condensed tomato soup

½ cup sliced green or ripe olives

¾ teaspoon salt

¼ teaspoon pepper

1 can (7.5 oz) Pillsbury refrigerated buttermilk or Country biscuits

1 egg, beaten

½ cup cornmeal

1 Heat oven to 375°F. In 10-inch skillet, cook beef, onion and bell pepper over medium heat 8 to 10 minutes, stirring occasionally, until beef is thoroughly cooked; drain. Stir in corn, soup, olives, salt and pepper; heat to boiling. Reduce heat; simmer uncovered while preparing biscuits.

2 Separate dough into 10 biscuits. Dip biscuits in egg, then cornmeal. Into ungreased shallow 1½-quart casserole or 9-inch square pan, spoon hot meat mixture. Top with coated biscuits.

3 Bake 20 to 30 minutes or until biscuits are golden brown.

High Altitude (3500–6500 ft): No change.

1 Serving: Calories 580; Total Fat 21g (Saturated Fat 6g; Trans Fat 1g); Cholesterol 125mg; Sodium 1940mg; Total Carbohydrate 70g (Dietary Fiber 5g) **Exchanges:** 3 Starch, 1½ Other Carbohydrate, 3 Lean Meat, 2 Fat **Carbohydrate Choices:** 4½

cheese-topped taco pie

6 SERVINGS

PREP TIME: *25 minutes*

START TO FINISH: *1 hour 20 minutes*

MICHELLE BOCIANSKI
Wheaton, IL
Bake-Off® Contest 35, 1992

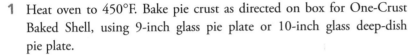

1 Heat oven to 450°F. Bake pie crust as directed on box for One-Crust Baked Shell, using 9-inch glass pie plate or 10-inch glass deep-dish pie plate.

2 Reduce oven temperature to 350°F. In 10-inch skillet, cook beef over medium-high heat 5 to 7 minutes, stirring frequently, until beef is thoroughly cooked; drain. Stir in taco seasoning mix and salsa. Heat to boiling. Reduce heat; simmer uncovered 5 minutes, stirring occasionally. Add mushrooms and half of the French-fried onions; mix well. Spoon mixture into baked pie shell.

3 In small bowl, mix ricotta cheese, 1 cup of the taco-seasoned cheese blend and the eggs. Spoon over beef mixture.

4 Bake at 350°F 25 to 35 minutes or until slightly puffed and set in center. Sprinkle remaining 1 cup cheese evenly over filling. Sprinkle remaining French-fried onions in center of filling. Bake 2 to 3 minutes longer or until cheese is melted.

5 Sprinkle tomato around edge and in center of filling. Let stand 10 to 15 minutes before serving.

High Altitude (3500–6500 ft): No change.

CRUST
1 Pillsbury refrigerated pie crust (from 15-oz box), softened as directed on box

FILLING
1 lb (at least 80%) ground beef

1 package (1 oz) taco seasoning mix

1 jar (16 oz) chunky-style salsa

1 jar (4.5 oz) sliced mushrooms, drained

1 can (2.8 oz) French-fried onions

1 cup ricotta cheese

2 cups shredded taco-seasoned cheese blend (8 oz)

2 eggs

1 small tomato, seeded, diced

1 Serving: Calories 630; Total Fat 41g (Saturated Fat 18g; Trans Fat 2.5g); Cholesterol 170mg; Sodium 1730mg; Total Carbohydrate 36g (Dietary Fiber 1g) **Exchanges:** 2 Starch, ½ Other Carbohydrate, 3½ Medium-Fat Meat, 4 Fat **Carbohydrate Choices:** 2½

turkey–sweet potato pot pies

DOLLY CRAIG
Denver, CO
Bake-Off® Contest 41, 2004

4 SERVINGS
PREP TIME: *15 minutes*
START TO FINISH: *55 minutes*

1 can (17 oz) vacuum-pack sweet potatoes, drained, cut into bite-size pieces (about 2½ cups)

1½ cups cubed cooked turkey or chicken

1 cup frozen sweet peas, thawed, drained

3 tablespoons chopped sweet yellow onion or onion

1 tablespoon curry powder

1 can (18.6 oz) ready-to-serve chicken pot pie style soup

Salt and pepper to taste, if desired

1 Pillsbury refrigerated pie crust (from 15-oz box), softened as directed on box

1 Heat oven to 400°F. In large bowl, mix all ingredients except pie crust. Divide mixture evenly among 4 (1¼- to 2-cup) ungreased individual ramekins.*

2 Unroll pie crust flat on work surface. Cut crust into 4 quarters. Top each filled ramekin with 1 quarter crust. With kitchen scissors or knife, trim crust edges. Pinch and flute edge, filling in areas with trimmed pie crust pieces where needed. With knife, cut several small slits in crusts for steam to escape. Place ramekins on cookie sheet.

3 Bake 25 to 33 minutes or until filling is bubbly and crust is deep golden brown, covering edge of crust with foil during last 10 to 15 minutes of baking to prevent excessive browning. Cool 5 minutes before serving.

*A 1¼- to 1½-quart casserole can be substituted for ramekins. Place whole crust over filled casserole. Do not place casserole on cookie sheet.

High Altitude (3500–6500 ft): No change.

1 Serving: Calories 490; Total Fat 18g (Saturated Fat 6g; Trans Fat 0g); Cholesterol 60mg; Sodium 800mg; Total Carbohydrate 61g (Dietary Fiber 5g) **Exchanges:** 2½ Starch, 1½ Other Carbohydrate, 2 Lean Meat, 2 Fat **Carbohydrate Choices:** 4

southwestern chicken-biscuit pot pie

DIANE LEIGH KEREKES
Sapulpa, OK
Bake-Off® Contest 42, 2006

2 SERVINGS
PREP TIME: *20 minutes*
START TO FINISH: *1 hour 10 minutes*

1 can (18.5 oz) ready-to-serve southwestern-style chicken soup

¼ teaspoon onion powder

¼ teaspoon garlic powder

¼ teaspoon ground chipotle chiles

Cooking spray

½ cup frozen extra-sweet whole kernel corn

1 package (3 oz) frozen diced cooked chicken (⅔ cup)

2 oz Monterey Jack cheese, cut into 4 (3 × 1 × ⅛-inch) slices

3 tablespoons chopped roasted red bell peppers (from jar)

2 Pillsbury Grands! Oven Baked frozen southern-style biscuits (from 25-oz bag)

2 to 4 tablespoons sour cream

1 to 2 tablespoons finely chopped fresh chives or green onions

1 Heat oven to 350°F. Pour soup into 2-cup measuring cup or bowl. Stir in onion powder, garlic powder and ground chipotle chiles.

2 Spray insides of 2 ovenproof 2-cup bowls with cooking spray. Place ¼ cup corn and ⅓ cup chicken in each bowl. Pour about 1 cup soup mixture evenly into bowls. Carefully place 2 cheese slices in center on top of soup in each bowl. Sprinkle 1 tablespoon roasted peppers evenly around cheese in each. Place biscuits over cheese; spray biscuits with cooking spray.

3 Place bowls on cookie sheet. Bake 38 to 43 minutes or until biscuits are golden brown and soup bubbles around edges. Cool 5 minutes before serving. Serve topped with sour cream, chives and remaining tablespoon roasted peppers.

High Altitude (3500–6500 ft): Bake 43 to 48 minutes.

1 Serving: Calories 570; Total Fat 26g (Saturated Fat 11g; Trans Fat 4.5g); Cholesterol 75mg; Sodium 1900mg; Total Carbohydrate 54g (Dietary Fiber 4g) **Exchanges:** 3 Starch, ½ Other Carbohydrate, 3 Lean Meat, 3 Fat **Carbohydrate Choices:** 3½

mexican beef pie

MRS. ALLEGRA BERNAL
Sylmar, CA
Bake-Off® Contest 21, 1970

6 SERVINGS

PREP TIME: *15 minutes*
START TO FINISH: *40 minutes*

1 lb lean (at least 80%) ground beef

1 package (1 oz) taco seasoning mix

½ cup water

⅓ cup sliced olives

1 can (8 oz) Pillsbury refrigerated
  crescent dinner rolls

1 cup crushed corn chips

1 container (8 oz) sour cream

1 cup shredded Cheddar cheese (4 oz)

1 cup corn chips

Shredded lettuce, if desired

Chunky-style salsa, if desired

1 Heat oven to 375°F. In 10-inch skillet, cook beef over medium-high heat 5 to 7 minutes, stirring frequently, until thoroughly cooked; drain. Stir in taco seasoning mix, water and olives. Reduce heat to low; simmer uncovered 5 minutes, stirring occasionally.

2 Meanwhile, separate dough into 8 triangles. Place triangles in ungreased 9-inch pie plate; press over bottom and up side to form crust. Sprinkle 1 cup crushed corn chips evenly in bottom of crust.

3 Spoon hot beef mixture over corn chips. Spread sour cream over beef mixture. Sprinkle with cheese and remaining 1 cup corn chips.

4 Bake 20 to 25 minutes or until crust is golden brown. Cut into wedges. Top with lettuce and salsa.

*To make the pie in advance, prepare it through step 3—except don't sprinkle with corn chips. Cover and refrigerate up to 2 hours. Sprinkle with corn chips; bake as directed.

High Altitude (3500–6500 ft): Bake 22 to 27 minutes. Cover edges of pie with foil during last 10 minutes of bake time.

1 Serving: Calories 560; Total Fat 39g (Saturated Fat 15g; Trans Fat 3g); Cholesterol 90mg; Sodium 1110mg; Total Carbohydrate 31g (Dietary Fiber 1g) **Exchanges:** 2 Starch, 2 Medium-Fat Meat, 5½ Fat **Carbohydrate Choices:** 2

breakfast quiches to go

16 QUICHES

PREP TIME: *25 minutes*
START TO FINISH: *45 minutes*

DIANE DENNY
Jacksonville, FL
Bake-Off® Contest 43, 2008

1 Heat oven to 350°F. Spray 16 regular size muffin cups with cooking spray.

2 Separate each can of dough into 8 triangles. Press 1 triangle over bottom and up side of each muffin cup.

3 In large bowl, beat cream cheese with electric mixer on medium speed until smooth. Add eggs, one at a time, beating well after each addition. Stir in onion, spinach, salt and pepper until well mixed. Fold in cheese. Fill each muffin cup to the top with egg mixture (do not overfill).

4 Bake 15 to 20 minutes or until knife inserted in center comes out clean and edges of rolls are golden brown. Remove from pan. Serve warm.

High Altitude (3500–6500 ft): Bake 18 to 23 minutes.

Photo on page 127.

2 cans (8 oz each) Pillsbury refrigerated crescent garlic butter dinner rolls (8 rolls each)
1 package (8 oz) cream cheese, softened
3 eggs
1 small onion, chopped (¼ cup)
1 box (9 oz) frozen spinach, thawed, squeezed to drain
¼ teaspoon salt
⅛ teaspoon pepper
1 cup shredded mozzarella cheese (4 oz)

1 Quiche: Calories 200; Total Fat 14g (Saturated Fat 6g; Trans Fat 1.5g); Cholesterol 55mg; Sodium 400mg; Total Carbohydrate 12g (Dietary Fiber 0g) **Exchanges:** 1 Starch, ½ Medium-Fat Meat, 2 Fat **Carbohydrate Choices:** 1

spinach, sausage and feta quiche

KATHLEEN HALLER
Baltimore, MD
Bake-Off® Contest 43, 2008

8 SERVINGS
PREP TIME: *30 minutes*
START TO FINISH: *1 hour 45 minutes*

1 Pillsbury refrigerated pie crust (from 15-oz box), softened as directed on box

½ cup finely crushed garlic and butter croutons

1 cup shredded Cheddar cheese (4 oz)

4 oz smoked turkey sausage, sliced

1 box (9 oz) frozen spinach, thawed, squeezed to drain and chopped

2 tablespoons finely chopped onion

1 cup crumbled feta cheese (4 oz)

4 eggs

1½ cups half-and-half

¼ teaspoon salt, if desired

⅛ teaspoon pepper

8 cherry tomatoes, cut into quarters

1 Heat oven to 350°F. Place pie crust in 9-inch glass pie plate or quiche pan as directed on box for One-Crust Filled Pie.

2 Cover bottom of pie crust with crushed croutons; sprinkle with Cheddar cheese. Layer sausage slices on cheese; top with spinach, onion and feta cheese.

3 In large bowl, beat eggs, half-and-half, salt and pepper with wire whisk until well blended; slowly pour into pie crust.

4 Bake 45 minutes. Cover edge of crust with strips of foil. Bake 5 to 15 minutes longer or until knife inserted in center comes out clean. Let stand 15 minutes before serving. Garnish with tomatoes.

High Altitude (3500–6500 ft): No change.

1 Serving: Calories 350; Total Fat 24g (Saturated Fat 12g; Trans Fat 0.5g); Cholesterol 145mg; Sodium 600mg; Total Carbohydrate 19g (Dietary Fiber 1g) **Exchanges:** ½ Starch, 1 Other Carbohydrate, 1½ Medium-Fat Meat, 3 Fat **Carbohydrate Choices:** 1

broccoli, potato and bacon quiche

TANYA NICOLE MARGALA
Newport Beach, CA
Bake-Off® Contest 42, 2006

8 SERVINGS
PREP TIME: *20 minutes*
START TO FINISH: *1 hour 5 minutes*

1 bag (19 oz) frozen roasted potatoes
with broccoli & cheese sauce

1 Pillsbury refrigerated pie crust
(from 15-oz box), softened as
directed on box

4 eggs

⅔ cup whipping cream

7 slices bacon, cooked, crumbled
(about ⅓ cup)

1 cup finely shredded Parmesan
cheese (4 oz)

1 cup finely shredded Cheddar
cheese (4 oz)

½ teaspoon dried basil leaves

½ teaspoon pepper

¼ teaspoon parsley flakes

⅛ teaspoon salt, if desired

1 teaspoon finely chopped fresh
chives

1 Heat oven to 350°F. Microwave frozen potatoes with broccoli & cheese sauce as directed on bag.

2 Meanwhile, place pie crust in 9-inch glass pie plate as directed on box for One-Crust Filled Pie.

3 In large bowl, beat eggs and whipping cream with wire whisk until well blended. Stir in cooked potato mixture and remaining ingredients except chives. Pour filling into crust-lined pie plate; spread evenly. Sprinkle chives over filling.

4 Bake 30 to 40 minutes or until edge of filling is light golden brown and knife inserted in center comes out clean. Let stand 5 minutes before serving.

High Altitude (3500–6500 ft): Heat oven to 375°F. Bake 33 to 43 minutes.

1 Serving: Calories 420; Total Fat 28g (Saturated Fat 14g; Trans Fat 0g); Cholesterol 170mg; Sodium 910mg; Total Carbohydrate 24g (Dietary Fiber 1g) **Exchanges:** 1½ Starch, 2 High-Fat Meat, 2 Fat **Carbohydrate Choices:** 1½

chicken enchilada quiche

JESSICA BARTON
Eugene, OR
Bake-Off® Contest 41, 2004

8 SERVINGS
PREP TIME: *15 minutes*
START TO FINISH: *1 hour 30 minutes*

1 Pillsbury refrigerated pie crust (from 15-oz box), softened as directed on box

4 eggs

1 cup half-and-half or milk

1 can (12.5 oz) chunk chicken breast in water, drained (1½ cups)

1½ cups broken tortilla chips

2 cups shredded Monterey Jack cheese (8 oz)

1 cup shredded Cheddar cheese (4 oz)

1 cup chunky-style salsa

1 can (4.5 oz) chopped green chiles

½ teaspoon salt

Pepper to taste, if desired

Sour cream, if desired

Additional salsa, if desired

1 Heat oven to 350°F. Place pie crust in 9- or 9½-inch glass deep-dish pie plate as directed on box for One-Crust Filled Pie.

2 In medium bowl, beat eggs with wire whisk until blended. Beat in half-and-half. Stir in chicken, chips, both cheeses, 1 cup salsa, the green chiles and salt. Pour into crust-lined pie plate. Sprinkle pepper over top of filling.

3 Bake 55 to 65 minutes or until crust is light golden brown and knife inserted in center comes out clean. Let stand 10 minutes before serving. Cut into wedges. Serve with sour cream and salsa,

High Altitude (3500–6500 ft): Heat oven to 375°F. After 15 minutes of baking in step 3, cover edges of crust with strips of foil to prevent excess browning.

1 Serving: Calories 590; Total Fat 38g (Saturated Fat 17g; Trans Fat 0g); Cholesterol 185mg; Sodium 1110mg; Total Carbohydrate 41g (Dietary Fiber 1g) **Exchanges:** 1 Starch, 2 Other Carbohydrate, 1 Medium-Fat Meat, 2 High-Fat Meat, 2½ Fat **Carbohydrate Choices:** 3

chicken-asiago-spinach quiche

WILL SPERRY

Bunker Hill, WV

Bake-Off® Contest 43, 2008

8 SERVINGS

PREP TIME: *30 minutes*

START TO FINISH: *1 hour 25 minutes*

1 Pillsbury refrigerated pie crust (from 15-oz box), softened as directed on box

2 tablespoons vegetable oil

½ teaspoon finely chopped garlic

1 medium onion, chopped (½ cup)

½ cup cooked real bacon pieces (from 2.5-oz package)

1 cup chopped cooked chicken

1 box (9 oz) frozen spinach, thawed, squeezed to drain and chopped

1 container (8 oz) sour cream

¼ teaspoon salt

¼ teaspoon garlic powder

⅛ teaspoon pepper

2 cups shredded sharp Cheddar cheese (8 oz)

1½ cups shredded Asiago cheese (6 oz)

3 eggs

½ cup whipping cream

1 Heat oven to 375°F. Bake pie crust as directed on box for One-Crust Baked Shell, using 9-inch glass pie plate or 9½-inch glass deep-dish pie plate. Cool on cooling rack 10 minutes.

2 Meanwhile, in 10-inch skillet, heat oil over medium heat. Add garlic and onion; cook 2 to 3 minutes, stirring occasionally, until onion is tender. Reduce heat. Stir in bacon, chicken and spinach; toss to combine. Remove from heat; transfer mixture to large bowl.

3 Stir sour cream, salt, garlic powder and pepper into spinach mixture until well blended. Stir in cheeses.

4 In small bowl, beat eggs and whipping cream with fork or wire whisk until well blended. Gently fold into spinach mixture until well blended. Pour filling into pie crust.

5 Bake 15 minutes. Cover edge of crust with strips of foil to prevent excessive browning. Bake 20 to 25 minutes longer or until center is set and edge of crust is golden brown. Let stand 15 minutes before serving.

High Altitude (3500–6500 ft): No change.

1 Serving: Calories 550; Total Fat 42g (Saturated Fat 21g; Trans Fat 0.5g); Cholesterol 185mg; Sodium 760mg; Total Carbohydrate 18g (Dietary Fiber 2g) **Exchanges:** 1 Starch, 3 Medium-Fat Meat, 5½ Fat **Carbohydrate Choices:** 1

italian zucchini crescent pie

MILLICENT (CAPLAN) NATHAN

Boca Raton, FL

Bake-Off® Contest 29, 1980

6 SERVINGS

PREP TIME: *30 minutes*

START TO FINISH: *1 hour*

2 tablespoons butter or margarine

4 cups thinly sliced zucchini

1 cup chopped onions

2 tablespoons parsley flakes

½ teaspoon salt

½ teaspoon pepper

¼ teaspoon garlic powder

¼ teaspoon dried basil leaves

¼ teaspoon dried oregano leaves

2 eggs, well beaten

2 cups shredded Muenster or mozzarella cheese (8 oz)

1 can (8 oz) Pillsbury refrigerated crescent dinner rolls

2 teaspoons yellow mustard

1 Heat oven to 375°F. In 12-inch skillet, melt butter over medium-high heat. Add zucchini and onions; cook and stir 6 to 8 minutes or until tender. Stir in parsley flakes, salt, pepper, garlic powder, basil and oregano.

2 In large bowl, mix eggs and cheese. Stir in cooked vegetable mixture.

3 Separate dough into 8 triangles. Place in ungreased 10-inch glass pie plate or 11-inch quiche pan*; press over bottom and up side to form crust. Firmly press perforations to seal. Spread crust with mustard. Pour egg mixture evenly into crust-lined pie plate.

4 Bake 18 to 22 minutes or until knife inserted near center comes out clean. Cover edge of crust with strips of foil during last 10 minutes of baking if necessary to prevent excessive browning. Let stand 10 minutes before serving.

*If you don't have a 10-inch glass pie plate or an 11-inch quiche pan, you can use a 12 × 8-inch (2-quart) glass baking dish or shallow 3-quart casserole. Unroll the dough into 2 long rectangles. Press the dough over bottom and one inch up sides of pan to form crust. Firmly press perforations to seal. Continue with recipe as directed.

High Altitude (3500–6500 ft): Bake 30 to 35 minutes, covering edge of crust with strips of foil after first 15 minutes of baking.

1 Serving: Calories 370; Total Fat 25g (Saturated Fat 13g; Trans Fat 2.5g); Cholesterol 115mg; Sodium 800mg; Total Carbohydrate 21g (Dietary Fiber 2g) **Exchanges:** 1 Starch, 1 Vegetable, 1½ High-Fat Meat, 2½ Fat **Carbohydrate Choices:** 1½

black bean and cheese tortilla pie

6 SERVINGS

PREP TIME: *20 minutes*

START TO FINISH: *1 hour 20 minutes*

DONNA BLANCERO

Ithaca, NY

Bake-Off® Contest 35, 1992

1 Heat oven to 350°F. Make pie crust as directed on box for Two-Crust Pie, using 9-inch glass pie plate or 10-inch glass deep-dish pie plate.

2 In 10-inch skillet, heat oil over medium-high heat until hot. Add onions and bell pepper; cook and stir about 5 minutes or until tender. Stir in beans, salsa, jalapeño peppers, chili powder and pepper; heat to boiling. Reduce heat; simmer uncovered 7 to 10 minutes, stirring occasionally.

3 Spoon about ½ cup bean mixture into crust-lined pie plate. Sprinkle with ½ cup of the cheese; top with tortilla. Repeat layering twice; sprinkle with remaining cheese. Top with second crust; seal edges and flute. Cut slits in several places in top crust.

4 Bake 40 to 50 minutes or until golden brown. Let stand 10 minutes before serving. Serve with sour cream.

High Altitude (3500–6500 ft): No change.

CRUST
1 box (15 oz) Pillsbury refrigerated pie crusts, softened as directed on box

FILLING
3 tablespoons vegetable oil

1 cup chopped onions

½ cup chopped green or red bell pepper

1 can (15 oz) black beans, drained, rinsed

½ cup chunky-style salsa

2 tablespoons finely chopped fresh jalapeño peppers, if desired

½ teaspoon chili powder, if desired

½ teaspoon ground red pepper (cayenne) if desired

2 cups shredded Cheddar cheese (8 oz)

3 flour tortillas (8 inch)

TOPPING
½ cup sour cream, if desired

1 Serving: Calories 710; Total Fat 40g (Saturated Fat 16g; Trans Fat 0.5g); Cholesterol 50mg; Sodium 800mg; Total Carbohydrate 70g (Dietary Fiber 9g) **Exchanges:** 1 Starch, 3½ Other Carbohydrate, 2 Medium-Fat Meat, 6 Fat **Carbohydrate Choices:** 4½

cheesy fiesta quiche

GRETCHEN KOCH
Rocky River, OH
Bake-Off® Contest 41, 2004

6 SERVINGS
PREP TIME: *25 minutes*
START TO FINISH: *1 hour 20 minutes*

CRUST

1 box (4.6 oz) white corn taco shells (12 shells)

3 tablespoons butter or margarine, melted

FILLING

3 eggs

1 cup small-curd cottage cheese

2 cups shredded Mexican cheese blend (8 oz)

½ cup milk

2 tablespoons butter or margarine, melted

⅓ cup Pillsbury BEST all-purpose flour

½ teaspoon baking powder

2 tablespoons chopped green chiles, drained (from 4.5-oz can)

2 tablespoons chopped ripe olives

TOPPING

6 tablespoons sour cream

6 tablespoons chunky-style salsa

1 Heat oven to 325°F. In food processor or blender, crush taco shells until very fine. In medium bowl, mix crushed taco shells and 3 tablespoons melted butter. Press over bottom and up side of 9-inch glass pie plate. Bake 15 minutes.

2 Meanwhile, in large bowl, beat eggs using whisk or fork. Add remaining filling ingredients except chiles and olives; beat with electric mixer on medium speed until well blended. Stir in chiles and olives.

3 Remove partially baked crust from oven; increase oven temperature to 400°F. Pour filling into crust.

4 Bake at 400°F 10 minutes. Reduce oven temperature to 325°F; bake 25 to 35 minutes longer or until center is slightly puffed and light golden brown. Cool 10 minutes.

5 Cut quiche into wedges; place on individual serving plates. Top each with 1 tablespoon sour cream and 1 tablespoon salsa. If desired, garnish plates with tortilla chips.

High Altitude (3500–6500 ft): Increase last bake time at end of step 4 to 30 to 40 minutes.

1 Serving: Calories 450; Total Fat 32g (Saturated Fat 17g; Trans Fat 2g); Cholesterol 180mg; Sodium 730mg; Total Carbohydrate 24g (Dietary Fiber 1g) **Exchanges:** 1½ Starch, 2 High-Fat Meat, 3 Fat **Carbohydrate Choices:** 1½

helpful nutrition and cooking information

Nutrition Guidelines

We provide nutrition for each recipe that includes calories, total fat, saturated fat, trans fat, cholesterol, sodium, total carbohydrate, dietary fiber, exchanges and carbohydrate choices. Individual food choices can be based on this information.

Recommended intake for a daily diet of 2,000 calories as set by the Food and Drug Administration

Total Fat	Less than 65g
Saturated Fat	Less than 20g
Cholesterol	Less than 300mg
Sodium	Less than 2,400mg
Total Carbohydrate	300g
Dietary Fiber	25g

Criteria Used for Calculating Nutrition Information

- The first ingredient was used wherever a choice is given (such as ⅓ cup sour cream or plain yogurt).

- The first ingredient amount was used wherever a range is given (such as 3- to 3-½–pound cut-up broiler-fryer chicken).

- Large eggs and 2% milk were used for testing.

- "If desired" ingredients and recipe variations were not included (such as sprinkle with brown sugar, if desired).

- The first serving number was used wherever a range is given (such as 4 to 6 servings).

- Only the amount of a marinade or frying oil that is estimated to be absorbed by the food during preparation or cooking was calculated.

Ingredients Used in Recipe Testing and Nutrition Calculations

- Fat-free, low-fat or low-sodium products were not used, unless otherwise indicated.

- Cooking spray or cooking spray with flour was used to grease pans, unless otherwise indicated.

Equipment Used in Recipe Testing

We use equipment for testing that the majority of consumers use in their homes. If a specific piece of equipment (such as a wire whisk) is necessary for recipe success, it is listed in the recipe.

- Cookware and bakeware without nonstick coatings were used, unless otherwise indicated.

- No dark-colored, black or insulated bakeware was used.

- When a pan is specified in a recipe, a metal pan was used; a baking dish or pie plate means ovenproof glass was used.

- An electric hand mixer was used for mixing only when mixer speeds are specified in the recipe directions. When a mixer speed is not given, a spoon or fork was used.

metric conversion guide

Volume

U.S. Units	Canadian Metric	Australian Metric
¼ teaspoon	1 mL	1 ml
½ teaspoon	2 mL	2 ml
1 teaspoon	5 mL	5 ml
1 tablespoon	15 mL	20 ml
¼ cup	50 mL	60 ml
⅓ cup	75 mL	80 ml
½ cup	125 mL	125 ml
⅔ cup	150 mL	170 ml
¾ cup	175 mL	190 ml
1 cup	250 mL	250 ml
1 quart	1 liter	1 liter
1½ quarts	1.5 liters	1.5 liters
2 quarts	2 liters	2 liters
2½ quarts	2.5 liters	2.5 liters
3 quarts	3 liters	3 liters
4 quarts	4 liters	4 liters

Weight

U.S. Units	Canadian Metric	Australian Metric
1 ounce	30 grams	30 grams
2 ounces	55 grams	60 grams
3 ounces	85 grams	90 grams
4 ounces (¼ pound)	115 grams	125 grams
8 ounces (½ pound)	225 grams	225 grams
16 ounces (1 pound)	455 grams	500 grams
1 pound	455 grams	0.5 kilogram

Measurements

Inches	Centimeters
1	2.5
2	5.0
3	7.5
4	10.0
5	12.5
6	15.0
7	17.5
8	20.5
9	23.0
10	25.5
11	28.0
12	30.5
13	33.0

Temperatures

Fahrenheit	Celsius
32°	0°
212°	100°
250°	120°
275°	140°
300°	150°
325°	160°
350°	180°
375°	190°
400°	200°
425°	220°
450°	230°
475°	240°
500°	260°

Note: The recipes in this cookbook have not been developed or tested using metric measures. When converting recipes to metric, some variations in quality may be noted.

index

Page numbers in *italics* indicate illustrations.

A

Asiago, -Chicken-Spinach Quiche, 146, *147*
Asparagus Ham Crescent Bake, 60

B

Bacon, Broccoli and Potato Quiche, 142, *143*
Baked Pork Chops with Biscuit Stuffin', 56
Barbecue Bake, Crescent, Easy-to-Make, 32, *33*
Beale Street Chicken Braid, 102
Bean(s)
    'n Beef Biscuit Casserole, 25
    'n Beef with Cheesy Biscuits, 12, *13*
    Biscuit Bake, Zesty, 14
    'n Frank Biscuit Casserole, 54, *55*
    and Franks Casserole, 52
    and Sausage Bake, 64
    White, and Chicken Bruschetta Bake, 88, *89*
    See also Black Bean
Beef
    Bake, Hearty Crescent, 35
    Bake, Spinach Crescent, 36
    'n Beans Biscuit Casserole, 25
    'n Beans with Cheesy Biscuits, 12, *13*
    Beefed-Up Biscuit Casserole, 21
    Biscuit 'n Corn Combo, 132
    'n Crescent Bake, Cheesy, 15
    Pie, Layered Italian, 129
    Pie, Mexican, 138
    'n Three Cheese Biscuit Casserole, 20
    See also Cheeseburger; Meatball; Roast Beef; Sloppy Joe;
        Steak

Big Tastin' Sloppy Joe Pie, 128
Biscuit Beef 'n Corn Combo, 132
Black Bean
    and Cheese Tortilla Pie, 149
    and Chicken Bake, 84
    -Pineapple Enchiladas, 116, *117*
    Tofu Enchiladas, 121
Breakfast Quiches to Go, *127*, 139
Broccoli
    Brunch Braid, 73
    -Cauliflower Tetrazzini, 122, *123*
    Potato and Bacon Quiche, 142, *143*

C

Caesar Salad, Chicken Squares, 100, *101*
California Casserole, 29
Calzones, Chicken Crescent, 95
Cauliflower, -Broccoli Tetrazzini, 122, *123*
Cheese
    and Black Bean Tortilla Pie, 149
    and Chicken Crescent Chimichangas, 91
    Chicken Enchiladas, 77
    and Crab Rolls, Deviled, 124, *125*
    'n Ham Omelet Bake, 62, *63*
    Steak Crescent Braids, 42, *43*
    Three, 'n Beef Biscuit Casserole, 20
    -Topped Taco Pie, 133
Cheeseburger
    Bake, Crescent, 34
    Casserole, 18
    Skillet, Chuck Wagon, 16, *17*

www.pillsbury.com

Cheesy
  Beef 'n Crescent Bake, 15
  Biscuit Chili Casserole, 19
  Biscuits, Beef 'n Beans with, 12, *13*
  Fiesta Quiche, 150, *151*
Chicken
  -Asiago-Spinach Quiche, 146, *147*
  Beale Street Braid, 102
  Biscuit Casserole, Crunchy, 82
  -Biscuit Pot Pie, Southwestern, 136, *137*
  and Black Bean Bake, 84
  Caesar Salad Squares, 100, *101*
  Caliente Crescent Casserole, 83
  Casserole, Fiesta, 94
  and Cheese Crescent Chimichangas, 91
  Cheese Enchiladas, 77
  Club, Rustic, 96
  Crescent Calzones, 95
  Empanada, Fiesta, 78
  Enchilada Pie, Speedy Layered, 80, *81*
  Enchilada Quiche, 144, *145*
  Manicotti Olé, 79
  Pie, Southwestern, 130, *131*
  Savory Crescent Squares, 97
  Savory Crust Bake, 87
  Suiza Cornbread Bake, 85
  Supper, Maryland, *75*, 76
  -Taco-Ranch Sandwiches, 98, *99*
  'n Vegetable Biscuit Bake, 86
  and White Bean Bruschetta Bake, 88, *89*
Chili, Biscuit Casserole, Cheesy, 19
Chimichangas, Chicken and Cheese
      Crescent, 91
Chuck Wagon Cheeseburger Skillet, 16, *17*
Chuckwagon Crescent Casserole, 37
Cod Bake, Crescent, 109
Corn
  Beef 'n Biscuit Combo, 132
  and Mushroom Brunch Squares, Quick, 74
  and Swiss Crescent Bake, 61

Cornbread, Chicken Bake, Suiza, 85
Crab
  and Cheese Rolls, Deviled, 124, *125*
  -in-a-Custard, 119
  Enchiladas, Cravin', 106, *107*
Crafty Crescent Lasagna, 58, *59*
Cravin' Crab Enchiladas, 106, *107*
Creole Crescent Shrimp Bake, 111
Crescent Cheeseburger Bake, 34
Crescent Cod Bake, 109
Crunchy Biscuit Chicken Casserole, 82

D

Deviled Crab and Cheese Rolls, 124, *125*

E

Easy Enchilada Bake, 11
Easy-to-Make Crescent Barbecue Bake,
      32, *33*
Empanada, Fiesta Chicken, 78
Enchilada(s)
  Bake, Easy, 11
  Chicken Cheese, 77
  Chicken Pie, Speedy Layered, 80, *81*
  Chicken Quiche, 144, *145*
  Crab, Cravin', 106, *107*
  Peanut Butter Mole, 92, *93*
  Pineapple–Black Bean, 116, *117*
  Shrimp, with Sweet Corn Sauce, 112, *113*
  Spinach and Mushroom with Creamy Red
      Sauce, 120
  Tofu Black Bean, 121

F

Feta, Sausage and Spinach Quiche, 140, *141*
Fiesta Chicken Casserole, 94
Fiesta Chicken Empanada, 78
Fiesta Taco Bake, 118
Frank 'n Bean Biscuit Casserole, 54, *55*
Franks and Beans Casserole, 52

G

Gnocchi Alfredo Casserole, 126
Golden Layers Biscuit Taco Casserole, 38, *39*
Grands! Roast Beef Sandwiches, 44, *45*

H

Ham
  Asparagus Crescent Bake, 60
  'n Cheese Omelet Bake, 62, *63*
  and Spinach Potato Casserole, 57
  and Swiss Crescent Braid, 68, *69*
  Swiss Ring-Around, 70, *71*
  'n Yam Biscuit Bake, 53
Hearty Crescent Beef Bake, 35
Hoagie Braids, Italian Meatball, 46, *47*
Hoagies, Mexi-Meatball, Toasted, 50
Hungry Boys' Casserole, 22, *23*

I

Italian
  Beef Pie, Layered, 129
  Casserole, Biscuit-Topped, 24
  Crescent Casserole, Zesty, 26, *27*
  Meatball Hoagie Braids, 46, *47*
  Zucchini Crescent Pie, 148

L

Lasagna, Crafty Crescent, 58, *59*
Layered Italian Beef Pie, 129
Louisiana Shrimp Bake, 114

M

Manicotti, Chicken Olé, 79
Maryland Chicken Supper, *75*, 76
Meatball, -Mexi Hoagies, Toasted, 50
Meatball Hoagie Braids, Italian, 46, *47*
Mexican
  Beef Pie, 138
  Crescent Bake, 31

Meatball Hoagies, Toasted, 50
  Tex-Mex Breakfast Bake, 66, *67*
Mushroom, and Corn Brunch Squares, Quick, 74
Mushroom, and Spinach Enchiladas with Creamy Red Sauce, 120

N

Neat-to-Eat Sloppy Joe Crescents, 48, *49*

O

Omelet Bake, Ham 'n Cheese, 62, *63*

P

Peanut Butter Mole Enchiladas, 92, *93*
Peppers. *See* entries under *Poblano*
Pineapple, –Black Bean Enchiladas, 116, *117*
Pizza, Crescent Casserole, 40
Pizza, Pop-Up Casserole, 41
Poblano Chile Peppers, Stuffed, 90
Poblano Florentine Casserole, *103*, 115
Pop-Up Pizza Casserole, 41
Pork Chops, Baked with Biscuit Stuffin', 56
Potato
  Broccoli and Bacon Quiche, 142, *143*
  Ham and Spinach Casserole, 57
  and Tuna Casserole, Scalloped, 105

Q

Quiche
  Breakfast, to Go, *127*, 139
  Broccoli, Potato and Bacon, 142, *143*
  Cheesy Fiesta, 150, *151*
  Chicken-Asiago-Spinach, 146, *147*
  Chicken Enchilada, 144, *145*
  Spinach, Sausage and Feta, 140, *141*
Quick Corn and Mushroom Brunch Squares, 74

R

Reuben in the Round Crescents, *51*, 72
Roast Beef, Sandwiches, Grands! 44, *45*
Rustic Chicken Club, 96

S

Salmon Fluff Casserole, 108
Sandwiches, Chicken-Taco-Ranch,
   98, *99*
Sandwiches, Grands! Roast Beef, 44, *45*
Sausage
  and Bean Bake, 64
  Crescent Braid, 65
  Spinach and Feta Quiche, 140, *141*
Savory Crescent Chicken Squares, 97
Savory Crust Chicken Bake, 87
Scalloped Tuna and Potato Casserole, 105
Seafood Fantasy, 110
Shrimp
  Bake, Creole Crescent, 111
  Bake, Louisiana, 114
  Enchiladas with Sweet Corn Sauce,
    112, *113*
Sloppy Joe, Crescents, Neat-to-Eat,
   48, *49*
Sloppy Joe Pie, Big Tastin', 128
Smoky Southwestern Shepherd's Pie, 28
Southwestern
  Chicken-Biscuit Pot Pie, 136, *137*
  Chicken Pie, 130, *131*
  Shepherd's Pie, Smoky, 28
Speedy Layered Chicken Enchilada Pie,
   80, *81*
Spinach
  Beef Crescent Bake, 36
  -Chicken-Asiago Quiche, 146, *147*
  and Ham Potato Casserole, 57
  and Mushroom Enchiladas with Creamy
    Red Sauce, 120
  Sausage and Feta Quiche, 140, *141*

Steak, Cheese, Crescent Braids, 42, *43*
Stuffed Poblano Chile Peppers, 90
Sweet Potato, -Turkey Pot Pies, 134, *135*
Swiss
  and Corn Crescent Bake, 61
  and Ham Crescent Braid, 68, *69*
  Ham Ring-Around, 70, *71*

T

Taco
  Bake, Fiesta, 118
  Biscuit Casserole, *9*, 10
  Biscuit Casserole, Golden Layers,
    38, *39*
  -Chicken-Ranch Sandwiches, 98, *99*
  Pie, Cheese-Topped, 133
Tamale Casserole, 30
Tasty Tuna Biscuit Casserole, 104
Tex-Mex Breakfast Bake, 66, *67*
Three Cheese 'n Beef Biscuit Casserole, 20
Toasted Mexi-Meatball Hoagies, 50
Tofu Black Bean Enchiladas, 121
Tortilla Pie, Black Bean and Cheese, 149
Tuna Biscuit Casserole, Tasty, 104
Tuna and Potato Casserole, Scalloped,
   105
Turkey-Sweet Potato Pot Pies, 134, *135*

V

Vegetable, 'n Chicken Biscuit Bake, 86

Y

Yam, 'n Ham Biscuit Bake, 53

Z

Zesty Biscuit Bean Bake, 14
Zesty Italian Crescent Casserole, 26, *27*
Zucchini, Crescent Pie, Italian, 148

meet the finalists

Alabama
Blevins-Russell, Paula, 90
Huff, Lisa, 100

Arizona
Flake, Jenny, 50, 98

Arkansas
Myers, Mandy, 102

California
Barnhart, Candace, 44
Bernal, Mrs. Allegra, 138
Chittock, Sharon, 106
Conway, Mrs. Ruth E., 119
Hatheway, Mrs. Hildreth H., 29
Joy, Cindy, 42
Margala, Tanya Nicole, 142
Rindone, Mrs. Kirsten H., 15
Rudolph, Mrs. Charla, 111
Weaver, Michael W., 124
Zebleckis, Marlene, 91

Colorado
Craig, Dolly, 134
Martinez, Margaret, 92

Connecticut
Fortier, Marjorie, 64
Francis, Mrs. Lyman, 70

Delaware
Fisher, Janielle, 78

Florida
Cappon, Mrs. Sally, 37
Denny, Diane, 139
Lee, Barbie, 77
Mathis, Harriet, 130
Mercer, Janet, 84
Nathan, Millicent (Caplan), 148
Wick, Robert, 24

Idaho
Tucker, Diane, 73

Illinois
Bocianski, Michelle, 133
Castle, Doris, 97
Klecka, Richard, 18
Sisson, Suzanne L.
   (Mrs. John W.), 31, 61
Vanni, Kristina, 28
Whitten, Mrs. C. B., 34

Indiana
Felts, Gloria, 115
Jackson, Mrs. Vyrla Kay, 35
Kube, Sharon, 96
Neyhouse, Mrs. Otto, 19
Rossell, Beverly, 46
Veasey, Mrs. Dorothy, 87

Iowa
Cox, Jill, 57
Hamilton, Karen, 10
Stafford, Claudia Lynn, 21

Kansas
Etherington, Joni, 65

Louisiana
Boudreaux, Ruth, 129
Feehan, Mrs. Mehrl D., 20

Maine
Pillsbury, Mrs. Brenda, 132

Maryland
Haller, Kathleen, 140
Huestis, Teresa, 76
Judy, Mrs. Betty, 25

Massachusetts
Santosuosso, Mrs. Virginia, 110

Michigan
Carrel, Mrs. Linda, 40
Davis, Louise V., 38
Nelson, Lori Ann, 85
Walilko, Mira, 22

Minnesota
Bathke, Madella, 26
Erickson, Mrs. Maureen, 14
Hall, Karen, 80
Iovinelli-Buescher, Mary, 116
Tripp, Gaile M. (Mrs. Jerry), 109

Missouri
Creed, Mrs. O. A., 12
Hahn, Barbara, 112
Hines, Evelyn, 30
Staufenbiel, Miss Amy, 11

Nebraska
Davis, Mrs. Lawrence C., 114
McWilliams, Renée, 79

New Jersey
Batich, Dennis, 54

New York
Blancero, Donna, 149
Demille, Mrs. Patricia, 36
Dorr, Kathy, 121
Maggio, Lorraine, 68
Van Doren, Mrs. Ann, 108
Van Itallie, Barbara, 122

North Carolina
Jennings, Carol, 83
Rader, Mrs. Geneva, 60

Ohio
Dunn, Mrs. Irene, 72
Koch, Gretchen, 150
Ohl, Mrs. Marion, 56

Oklahoma
Barson, Mrs. Mary, 104
Kerekes, Diane Leigh, 136

Oregon
Barton, Jessica, 144

Pennsylvania
DeSantis, Mrs. Shirley A., 53
Jackson, Phoebe, 118
Stavish, Miss Monica, 32

South Carolina
Kohn, Shannon, 88

Texas
Billingsley, Margie, 95
Hill, Robin, 120
Huber, Helen, 74
Milliron, Lynne, 66
Taylor, Betty, 58

Utah
Evans, Mrs. Nancy, 86

Virginia
Vaughan, Mrs. William, 52

Washington
Amberson, Julie, 62
Baxter, Kelly Lynne, 126
Byam, Shirlie M. (Mrs. Ben), 41
Schrag, Rhoda, 48
Sullivan, Mrs. Brian L., 128

West Virginia
Sperry, Will, 146
Warmuth, Rosemary, 16

Wisconsin
Carlson, Mrs. Margaret, 105
Harschutz, Laurene, 94
Miller, Mrs. Martin, 82